MENTAL ILLNESS

The Silent Pandemic

Dianne Lackey Benedict

TWO CAROLYNS PRESS
Nashville, TN

Dedication

This book is dedicated to my brother,
Donald Enoch Lackey,
who was diagnosed with chronic schizophrenia at the
age of eighteen and has triumphantly lived with this
disease all these years. He is now seventy-two. I love
you, Donald.

Contents

Foreword

Carolyn Benedict Fraser | *December 3, 2020*

My mother, Dianne Benedict, was forty years old when she had me in 1984. At this time my dad, Buddy, had recently graduated from the Divinity School at Vanderbilt University. When I was born, they were in the middle of a career change for my dad which was a significant life adjustment. They were also in the middle of raising my three older siblings — Andy and Fran were ten-year-old twins, and my oldest sister, Elysabeth, was thirteen.

I had the great fortune of entering a household where childhood was considered the most important and significant stage of life. This was due to my mother. She was determined to treat us not like children "who have a lot to learn," but as individuals with the unmatched intelligence of instinct and intuition on our side. She treated us as people with valid needs and desires.

As I got older, I realized that my mother's attitude towards childhood and towards raising us was uncommon. I noticed that the rest of society seemed to think that the significance of each life stage increased with age. Society told us that we were to work our way up the ladder from primary to secondary education, to college or other achievements, and not until we landed in a career could our identity solidify and our life be taken seriously.

My mother thought about this the other way around. She believed that if children were taken seriously, and childhood was treated like the fertile soil that it was, our identity would be firmer early on. And when, as adults, we met the inevitable challenges and struggles that life presented us, we would be able to manage them with more confidence and grace. She believed that a nurtured childhood is the grease of life – it makes all the parts work the way they were meant to and, as a result, life requires less maintenance in the end.

For our family, she created a world of believing. She believed me if I said I was not feeling well and needed to stay home from school. If I became angry, she wouldn't talk me out of it or punish me, she believed my anger and trusted that it came from a legitimate place and had a chain of needs, fears, and desires attached to it.

She believed in taking "Mental Health Days" decades before it became a hashtag and was built into corporate language. She believed that we could get through just about anything if we tried. Her philosophy was simple – because she believed in herself, she believed us, and because of that, we believed in ourselves. I can't think of a greater gift a parent could give to their child.

You might say that my mom was born to raise children; that she has a God-given ability to care for and nurture the people around her. Yes, her ability to connect to people, especially children, is undeniable, but to say that this is what she was made to do oversimplifies who she is. When she was growing up, many considered it a woman's role to care for and tend to their children. To say that my mom was responding to those generational expectations would also be oversimplifying her.

My mom had the God-given ability to care for and nurture the people around her not because it was hardwired into her soul, but because she chose to prioritize it. She dedicated her time and energy to understanding the complexity of caring for others and understood that the role begins with caring for herself. Behind every role she fills and every action she takes, there is commitment, passion, fire, and grit behind it.

Her life philosophy didn't happen by coincidence. It wasn't miraculously bestowed upon her. Though she is a devout Christian and has gained a lot of insight from church, this philosophy did not solely originate there either. It wasn't taught to her by a friend, parent, or sibling. A philosophy as deep, steady, and interwoven as Mom's came about in a more complex way — through her natural curiosity and desire to blend spiritual and psychological inputs, through her bravery and inclination to be an assertive woman, and through the determination and foresight to alter her actions so that she could positively impact the world for her offspring and her offspring's offspring, and so on.

Our cherished family psychologist once told her that the greatest beneficiary of her therapy would not be her, but her grandchildren. This profound idea — which resists the immediacy that this fast-paced, technologically-advanced world demands of us — has been the guiding force of her adulthood and is the central concept of this book.

At 36-years-old, I am approaching the age my mom was when she had me, and I am deeply honored to have had the opportunity to edit this book. Initially, I considered this task similar to following a recipe. I knew it would involve a lot of ingredients, but if we followed the right steps, it would be a straightforward process. But after a while it occurred to me that we weren't the cooks, we were the ingredients. She, and consequently her family, were what the story was made of. Because of this, the process of writing the book was more complex, more intimate, and ultimately more rewarding than I ever imagined it would be.

In this memoir and call-to-action book, my mother lays out her life story, her convictions towards mental health advocacy, and proclaims her view that we, as a global community, are in the midst of a mental health crisis. She has been quietly accumulating the contents of her story for fifteen years. Speaking for every member of our family, we could not be more grateful to be bystanders and beneficiaries of the contents of this book. Because of this, we thank you, Mom, Dede, Dianne — you are more than a mother, a wife, and a grandmother; you are a friend, a confidant, and a resounding inspiration.

Dianne & Carolyn, 2015

Acknowledgements

First and foremost, I am indebted to my youngest daughter and namesake, Carolyn Lackey Benedict Fraser, her husband, Rory Fraser, and my long time friend, Rosann White Smothers. At my request, these three helped me write and edit my book; their writing and computer skills far surpass mine. I knew that I could not write it alone. The biggest plus is that they understand the message I am trying to convey. Thanks, Carolyn, Rory, and Rosie.

Precious Marcia Fraser, my son-in-law, Rory's, Mother, has helped me and Carolyn with Pressbooks. Without her, this book might not exist.

Thank you, to my husband, Buddy, and our other three children — Elysabeth (Beth), Andy, and Fran — for encouraging Carolyn and me all along the way.

The crown jewels in my life, my Grandchildren, Khullun (Beth and Guy's son), Andrew, Michael, and Kirsten (Andy and Jen's children). I love you as much as all the stars in the heavens, all the grains of sand at the oceans, all the raindrops and snowflakes that fall from the sky, all the leaves on the trees, and all the blades of grass on the ground and more.

Thank you, Dr. Ted Morton, my Dynamic Psychotherapist, who has enabled me "to fly." Thank you to those who have been my therapists after Dr. Morton retired. Their objectivity and expertise are invaluable to me.

Thank you to the theologians, who have enabled me to have mainstream and well-balanced spiritual development over the years. In addition, thank you to the churches and Sunday School classes and teachers that have provided a spiritual community for me and my family.

My deepest appreciation to my siblings who have supported our parents' wishes, without question, in regard to taking care of our brother, Donald, who developed chronic schizophrenia when he was eighteen. A special thanks to my brother, Joe Lackey, who has served our family pro bono in all of our legal endeavors, and my sisters, Betty Blythe Lackey Wilson, Fran Lackey Clippard, and Fran's husband, Scooter, who coordinated all early efforts in starting The Center for Living and Learning Nashville in Franklin, TN (a residential care center for adults with schizophrenia and bipolar disorders). Fran and Scooter, the CLLN Board of Directors, and the CLLN Staff are at the helm today. George, John, and Tim Gianikas and their family, our Blythewood Joint Venture partners, who have financially and emotionally supported our family and the Center over the years.

Last, but certainly not least, thank you to the athletes who have helped me be healthy and physically fit – my tennis coaches and my son, Andy Benedict, who is my personal trainer. And to my daughters, Fran, and Elysabeth who help me with nutrition, fitness, meditation, balance, and of course love.

Unfortunately, at the moment, the COVID-19 Pandemic is happening. However, I have to give it some credit for slowing me down enough to finish my book. This is a very scary and difficult time for our world. I hope and pray that I live to see my book published.

Dianne Lackey Benedict
Nashville, TN
January 2021

1

Never Mind -The Disease No One Talks About

Every day in the broadcast news, we get the figures. Every time we pick up a newspaper, we see the numbers. Coronavirus-19 and its chilling statistics are right in front of our eyes. The Vietnam War took fewer lives, or so the stats say. No doubt at all – the COVID-19 pandemic of 2020 is a killer and is acceptable fodder for headlines. But, it is not alone in its ability to kill, maim, and ruin lives. In fact, it has a worthy opponent that has been around much, much longer, has cost more lives, and is almost never the subject of a news headline. That ugly, ruthless competitor is mental illness.

According to statistics, one in every five Americans will be affected by some form of mental illness in their lifetime. The big difference between these persons and in COVID-19 victims, veterans with war injuries, and any other persons with crippling or life-altering diseases can be summed up in one word — silence. Trust me, you won't hear someone tell you over lunch about going to psychiatric care. Those with affected family members won't level with their children about what is really wrong with Aunt Sally in the sanitarium or why Grandpa took his own life.

Because we have played it safe on the subject of mental illness for so long, we have created an atmosphere of distrust, denial, and fear. And, even more dangerously, we have made mental illness such a taboo that people who seriously need help often don't get it. An extreme example of this was evidenced a few years ago here in the Nashville, Tennessee area. A father gave guns to a son who had a history of mental issues, and then the son proceeded to take the lives of several innocent people at a local restaurant.

This same pattern has been played out time and time again in so-called "mass shootings." Almost every time, the perpetrator has been identified as a person who has suffered from some form of mental illness. And, of course, this has made a good case for gun legislation. But what about mental health reform? Where are the voices crying out for more openness and honesty about this widespread disease? Obviously, for a person with a very disturbed mind, packing a gun is not just a gun issue. I personally feel that war-designed weapons of mass destruction have no more place in the hands of an average citizen than Sherman tanks driving down interstates. Until we seriously address the subject of mental illness, we will continue to see its cruel effects on society.

If you are wondering why I am so invested in mental illness, the answer is simple: I have been there. It is a problem I have confronted personally in my own life and the lives of several members of my family. Because of my experience, I believe that we should care for our own minds with the same intent that we would care for a child or anything else of extreme value.

Over the past decades and even centuries, the worldwide lack of attention and lack of action in dealing with mental health issues has resulted in what I refer to as a "Global Mental Health Crisis." In my opinion, this crisis can also be referred to as a pandemic, analogous to the COVID-19 disease we are unfortunately experiencing now. Both diseases are negatively affecting all aspects of our lives. Over time, the negative and subtle stigmas and taboos associated with mental health and mental illness have saturated and controlled a large percentage of the minds and actions of our world population. International and domestic terrorism also come to mind.

So what do we do about this alarming mess? I think we – in our country and in many parts of the world – must take the lead and make some radical decisions that value real emotional well-being in our societies. Maybe the COVID-19 pandemic will slow our world down long enough, for us to take the time to reassess our value systems. I find that in the traditional structures of individual development, our country's priorities have been centered primarily around excellence in academics, athletics, politics, and religious commitment. To give some standard to monitor our emotional growth as individuals and society at large, we have been using these structures as frameworks of understanding to address our mental health needs. Unfortunately, genuine mental health development has become stunted, secondary, or even non-existent.

We must dig deeper and make dramatic changes. Through my experience, over the seventy-seven years of my life, I have found that this model, described above, is no longer sufficient in meeting the current needs we have in our society and world. Instead of emotional wellness being the result of our academic, physical, and religious aptitudes, we need to concentrate our attention on an undiluted, intentional focus as it pertains to emotional wellness and mental health education. The stigmas associated with mental illnesses have created an almost insurmountable degree of fear whether we realize it or not. Many will not even consider seeking professional psychological help due to subconscious fears that have existed over centuries. Some will claim that God is their therapist, thus avoiding the emotional, mental, and spiritual assistance tools that God created for us to use in the first place. Without a doubt, God is one of my therapists along with my clinical psychotherapist, whom I talk with once a month or more when needed. Theology and Psychology have been competing with each other for, heaven knows, way too long. In my opinion, the two "ologies" need to be more inclusive and work together in order to maintain a healthy and well-balanced society.

I will never understand how gun control has been neglected after the massacre of innocent kindergarteners at Sandy Hook Elementary School and the disproportionate gunning down of black Americans by our racist and bigoted population, including some of our own police. This must not be rationalized or allowed to continue. I have lost count of the number of times a mass shooting has occurred and mental illness is labeled as the cause. We then hear very little about anyone investigating what needs to be done. Mental illness is stigmatized. We are afraid to get close to it, to pinpoint it, to touch it, or even speak about it. But in order to prevent and treat mental illness, we must directly confront it. Stigmas develop over time. Adults experience stigmas, but children do not. Adults experience stigmas because they have lived long enough to learn them. Children haven't lived long enough to be afraid of mental illness. Because of this, it is essential that we integrate mental health awareness into our education systems. We must intervene in order to prevent our youth from developing fears associated with mental health as they grow into adulthood. So, how do we confront these stigmas? How do we confront our fears?

Let's talk about it in our schools, from early childhood development to high school students. Let's design an age-appropriate psychological curriculum to ensure, as much as possible, the development of a healthy sense of self-worth for each student. Children spend as many hours in school as they do at home, if not more. Academic and athletic excellence would become natural by-products of an intentional, positive emotional foundation in our educational system. A strong team of psychiatrists, clinical psychologists, parents, students, school counselors, teachers, and the National/International Departments of Education, all need to work together in order to create a foundational educational environment conducive to mental health development beginning in the area of a young child's self-confidence, self-worth, and self-esteem. This is a big inside-out endeavor that all global societies need to ponder and act upon expeditiously. Can we? Or are we like deer in headlights – subconsciously paralyzed and frozen by stigmas? When are we going to wake up and begin the process of redirecting and turning around this distorted, destructive, downward spiral? All of the above will take a "world village."

The actress Goldie Hawn developed MINDUP, a school program for children's brain health. The program offers techniques that manage emotions and behaviors through mindfulness practices. This program can dovetail right into the age-appropriate curriculum I am referring to.

Mental dis-ease is unseen or invisible like cancer inside the body. I think I finally understand why the prophet Jesus made the statement, "God, forgive them, for they do not understand what they are doing." It is time that we understand what we are doing or not doing. The fears associated with the hidden stigmas of mental illness have been all-consuming for too long — in the past and in the present. These fears are breeding extreme behaviors that result in racism, suicide, sexual abuse, domestic violence, mass killings, substance abuse such as over-use of alcohol, and prescription drug addictions. Also, religious fanaticism and sexual and gender discrimination abound. The list is endless. I'm talking about an unprecedented mental health emphasis beginning with building the self-worth of humankind from the ground up. Maybe this sounds like pie-in-the-sky for some, but a revolutionary mental health transformation can be a reality. It must to be a reality. Once we begin to value and cultivate a positive sense of self-worth in children and intentionally seek out help to improve our own self-worth and self-confidence as adults, I believe we will then have the ability to free ourselves from what is plaguing us and therefore plaguing our world. Let's get started. This can happen.

2

All In the Family

Before moving forward, you need to understand where I'm coming from. My upbringing is central to the concept of this book.

I was born on December 18, 1943, to Elysabeth and Joseph Lackey in Nashville, Tennessee. My childhood was relatively normal or seemed so to me. I was one of seven children. My six brothers and sisters are Joe Jr., Betty, John, Donald, Fran, and Thomas. Most people thought we were Catholic because there were so many kids in our family. There were many advantages. We always had someone to play with, which I found to be an advantage of growing up in a large family. We never had a problem getting a good baseball or tag football game going in our front yard. Plus, neighborhood kids usually wanted to join in. We lived at 3510 Hillsboro Road in Green Hills and were surrounded by wonderful neighbors.

My mom was a beautiful woman and quite prim and proper. She was always at home and there for us; however, she was depressed a lot. Physically, she was there, but sometimes not there mentally and emotionally. Mom's escape from depression was having kids and staying busy with our activities. She actually said that going to the hospital for two weeks to have a baby was the best vacation she ever had. No wonder she had seven children.

Mother would either give me credit or blame me, depending on her state of mind, for having four children after me. "The reason I had four children after you, was because you were so sweet and such a good baby," she would say to me. I was her inspiration to have more children, for better or for worse. I took it as a compliment.

The Lackey Family in the side yard at 3510 Hillsboro Road, 1955
Left to right: Me, Betty, Donald, Dad, Thomas, Mom, Fran, Joe, John

When Mom became really angry at us, she would throw out a high-pitched scream. I can remember her having a chair in our side yard where she would go sit alone and try to collect herself. Oddly enough, she did not remember all the screaming. She just remembered loving and enjoying us.

"I wish I were dead!" she would sometimes say when she lost her temper. I did not like her screaming and saying that. It really scared me.

Mom got her driver's license when I was about ten years old. She was forty. One day, she told us kids, that she was taking us on a ride and instructed us to get in the car. I ran upstairs and called my dad at his office to see if it were okay to go with her, or to see if she had lost her mind. I was afraid that she was going to drop us off somewhere, like Hansel and Gretel's dad did, or like my dad dropped off our two dogs in the country because they had killed some of our chickens.

According to Dad, she had passed her driver's test the week before and assured me that we were safe in her hands, even with her hands on the wheel. Reluctantly, I went back downstairs with my other nervous siblings, thinking it might be our last day on earth. Needless to say, we survived the ride, and Mom was one happier woman knowing how to drive and get away from home.

My Dad was a handsome lawyer and spent most of his time working to make enough money to support our large family. At least that is what I thought until Mom told me in my early teens that working hard for the family wasn't all he spent his time doing. He also spent his time having an affair.

One night, Mom had a friend of hers follow Dad home from work, but instead of coming straight back home, he went to another woman's apartment.

All of us were afraid of our Dad to one degree or another. Sometimes, in his anger, he would physically and verbally abuse us, especially the boys. Fortunately, he was away from home a lot of the time. In hindsight though, I wished a non-abusive version of him was around more. I needed a father. I wanted a gentle father.

Sometimes, we would act up and fight at home and Mom would threaten us by saying she was going to call Dad at his office if we didn't stop. This was how things worked at that time. Traditional gender roles were alive and well, especially in the South. It was an unspoken rule that we all deferred to Dad. He had the first and last word.

When Mom called him at work concerning our upheavals at home, he would get irate. His anger would churn and gain momentum during the day as we prepared ourselves to be "switched" with a twig from a bush or belted when he arrived. To make it worse, we had to go outside and select the switch we were going to be switched with. Occasionally he would forget and not do anything, or get home too late. But, if the misbehavior was severe enough, we knew he would not forget.

As I see it, Dad escaped his stresses by working late hours, having an affair, and being verbally abusive to Mom and to us. That being said, Dad never hit Mom, but that didn't make it hurt less. His abuse towards her was emotional and verbal.

Thankfully as an adult, I have found ways to come to terms with his anger.

Mom told him that if he ever hit her, she would leave. I want to believe that, and I do. Knowing that she had a line that couldn't be crossed made me feel stronger and taught me a lesson in self-respect.

Dad would throw objects at the wall and scare the hell out of us when he was overly angry. He would say "God Damn" and curse a lot when he was mad. I thought it was a terrible thing to say and still do. It was a great disrespect to God and for those listening. Needless to say, going to church was certainly not a top priority for Dad. He would occasionally go with our family, but usually on Sunday mornings, burning the trash took precedence.

It is important for me to express that Dad was not all bad. He had many good qualities. He was kind and loving lots of the time and worked hard to support our family the best that he could. I think Dad especially loved me. I do not know why, but he did, and I knew it. I wish all my siblings felt that he loved them just as much, but I do not think they did.

Even though Mom and Dad had their hang-ups, they loved us. I just wish they could have loved themselves as individuals and one another more.

Because of the instability of my parent's relationship, my older sister, Betty, and my older brother, Joe, were probably given too much responsibility too early in life. They helped our parents take care of the rest of us. Culturally, boys were considered more important than girls, and we accepted it because there wasn't anything telling us differently. The tension of gender roles created rivalry and jealousy, especially between Betty and Joe, my oldest siblings.

Aside from my parents and siblings, there was an essential person that was always there for us; she was our rock, Alice Sloss. I first met Alice when I was seven years old, and she was twenty-three. Alice worked for my Dad's parents after graduating from high school and came to work for our family after they died. She was a godsend. She came to our home five days a week and helped us with ironing, cooking, and cleaning. Alice could really sing, and she would sing her church choir gospel songs while she worked. When she realized we were listening, she would get embarrassed and stop.

Alice did not like it when we kids would fight. Usually, she would stay out of the way and pretend that she did not hear us. But, when things got out of control, she would holler at us to stop fighting, and we knew she meant business. Her contagious laughter and sense of humor were two of her most valuable assets. Honesty was another. She told us that her mother had instilled in her the importance of honesty, and she wanted us to be the same way. "Al" is the nickname we gave her. Al was an angel in our midst. Her faith, her family, extended family (us), and her church family were of utmost importance to her. We would visit her church on special occasions, and we were always warmly accepted. She had an electrifying smile and a contagious laugh. I am sure that she had her faults, but they were well hidden, whatever they were. In the dysfunctions of our home, she brought love, hope, and laughter, which we all related to and needed. Al was a "soul sister," a surrogate Mother and Grandmother, and a friend to our family all rolled into one. Thank you God for Al and Thank you, Al.

Al and I, 2014

Remember the classic song written and sung by Paul McCartney and Stevie Wonder? "Ebony and Ivory live together in perfect harmony, side by side on my piano keyboard, oh Lord, why don't we?" Well, Al and I did as best as we could, and I am thankful.

One quote that Al would always say, "God may not be on my time, but God is always on time." She truly believed it with all of her heart and soul. So do I.

Al passed away in the summer of 2016. She had been sick but was recovering. We had planned to go see her when we returned from a trip to Florida, but she passed away in her sleep while we were away. Our family attended her wake at the Church of the Living God and thanked her and her family for all she had given us. We sang and sang with her church sisters and brothers and gave her a good send off to heaven.

~

Ever since I was a small child, going to church was a priority. I am thankful that my mom had the vision and understanding of its importance. Fortunately, for the most part, I had positive experiences in the churches we attended. As a toddler, Russell Street Church of Christ was my first introduction to church. My mother's mother, Granny, lived up the street and attended there with us. My grandfather, Bye-Bye Daddy was not a church attendee, he was an engineer for the L & N (Louisville and Nashville) railroad. We had to say "bye" to him a lot as he was always leaving home on the train, so that is how he got his nickname. "Bye, Bye Daddy." He and Granny divorced before I got to know him.

Mom had a way of making sure that church was "walking accessible" when she could not drive. The Church of Christ, down the street, was strict and conservative. There was music without musical instruments during the worship service. We would sing the hymns a cappella with a song leader. Somewhere in the Bible, there is mention of no musical instruments being used in church, and that particular church interpreted the Bible literally. Fortunately, I was too young to know how narrow the doctrine was.

Russell Street Church of Christ, 1948
Far left, second row – Betty and I holding hands

When I was six years old, our family outgrew the house in East Nashville. Mom and Dad found a home, that would fit all of us, in the Green Hills community on the other side of the Cumberland River in South Nashville. We were surrounded by all kinds of churches — United Methodist, Disciples of Christ, and Baptist. All were right across the street.

My first choice and first attempt to find a church did not work out very well. The prettiest and closest one, Woodmont

Christian Church, had an enormous steeple that reached to the heavens. If Mom got lost while driving us around, she would use the steeple to find her way back home. One Sunday morning when I was six years old, I got dressed in dressy clothes that I had picked out, took the pink sponge rollers out of my hair, and put on my freshly painted and polished white shoes. All this preparation I did the night before. Church, God, and Jesus were my top priorities. Mom prepared my breakfast of fresh eggs from our hen house, bacon, toast with jelly, and O.J. When I finished eating, Mom and I walked to the end of our driveway, and she watched me cross the road. Since she needed to get back to the rest of the family, she did not go with me.

As I walked toward the huge steeple, it got taller and taller, and I got smaller and smaller. I was greeted by a church member at the large, dark green, front double doors. He directed me to find a seat amidst the congregation. Since I did not have anyone familiar to sit with, I began to feel a little nervous and self-conscious about being there alone.

The service began, and the minister asked all the visitors to stand up and introduce themselves. I stood up (all four feet of me), and the next thing I knew, I was surrounded by laughter. The congregation found it cute and humorous that a young girl would be visiting their church all by herself, but I did not think it was a laughing matter. Just moments earlier, I had been so excited to be there, and then, in a split second, I found myself so embarrassed and humiliated. I could not wait to go back home. I told myself I'd never go back, and I didn't.

At some point after that, the pastor, Brother Blue, from Calvary Methodist Church, called us and wanted to pay our family a visit. Calvary was directly across the street and was my second choice. We were so appreciative, honored, and excited that Brother Blue would come to our home. Our meeting with him went well, and we all decided to attend the worship service the next Sunday.

A few Sundays later, our family of nine, lined up in front of the congregation and joined the church. It couldn't have been more convenient. All we had to do was walk across the street to attend the events we were interested in. There were Sunday School classes, followed by a worship service in the sanctuary, summer Vacation Bible School (juice and cookie snack served), choirs to join, Christmas pageants and caroling (hot chocolate and Krispy-Kreme doughnuts were served to warm us up), M.Y.F. (Methodist Youth Fellowship group), dances, loving and caring people, learning about Jesus and God, etc. All across the street! The church became a home away from home and a safe haven for me from the second grade through high school — a safe haven from the dysfunction within my own home. Our family was so fortunate. The church's message of love, acceptance, and forgiveness was a major influence on me during those formative years.

I loved the church because of all of the reasons above, but I also loved it because I could flirt with the cute boys. During one of our high school choir rehearsals, I was accused by the youth choir director who said, "Dianne, I think the only reason you come to choir practice is to flirt with the boys." Granted, I probably was talking too much. He made this proclamation in front of the whole high school choir. I was embarrassed and swore I would never go back, but I did because I loved to sing, I wanted to learn about Jesus and God, I wanted to be with my church friends, and because, of course, I wanted to flirt with the boys!

3

Extended Family

The late fifties and early sixties were troublesome times. Our new minister, Sam Johnson, found himself amid the racial segregation crisis. One Sunday morning, during the worship service, he announced to our congregation that he would not turn anyone away from the front doors of our church, regardless of the color of their skin.

As a result, the church split. The "conservative" segregationists bought property down the street, and the "liberal" integrationists stayed put. Our family stayed and supported Dr. Johnson. He was an exceptional man and walked in several of the civil rights marches in downtown Nashville. He was way ahead of his time. Our congregation was so fortunate that he was our minister during such a volatile period. I cringe when I think of how difficult the struggle was for him and his family.

Evidence of the racial unrest also showed up at home. One Christmas Eve, Mom and Dad and some of us kids were returning from the annual trip to the country where we picked up two cakes made by a black woman, who was one of Dad's clients. Dad would barter with his clients if they could not pay their legal fees. The cakes fell into this category. One cake was a yellow sheet cake covered with fluffy white icing and loaded with freshly shaved coconut. The other was a round, double-layered spice cake with homemade caramel icing. The aroma of freshly baked cakes filled our car. We looked for Santa Claus, Rudolph, and the reindeer in the black, starlit sky, trying to wait patiently for our piece of cake and a glass of ice-cold milk when we got home. As we got closer to home, we noticed something burning in our side yard. It was a large wooden, burning cross. My siblings and I had no idea what was going on, and we thought it was pretty. Mom and Dad were very quiet and made few comments. It took me getting a little older to understand that the Ku Klux Klan had visited us. To this day, I do not know whether it was because we did not leave our church with the "conservative segregationists" or because of Dad's kindness to his African American clients who could not afford his legal fees. Maybe and probably both.

~

When I was eight years old, another traumatic event happened that took time for me to understand more deeply. I have a memory of a neighborhood playmate fondling me. At the time, I liked it and thought it felt good. One day though, he got angry at me because I did not want to join in playing capture the flag with our neighborhood friends. He threatened to tell them that I let him touch my private parts if I did not play. I was extremely embarrassed and devastated at the thought. This was my first bad experience with sex and sexuality. That experience made an indelible negative mark on how I would feel about sexuality in future years. I see now, with the help of my therapist, that this was a form of sexual and emotional abuse that distorted my understanding of sex. Many years later a sex therapist told me that the boy would now be considered a predator who had, more than likely, been sexually abused himself. What made it even more impactful was that at that time, sexuality was taboo. My parents did not talk about sexual matters, even though they had seven kids. So, by a process of deduction, sex seemed bad or wrong. Intercourse was not a vocabulary word in my family. Not even a word that came close or was in the vicinity – penis, vagina, puberty, were all unmentionable, and therefore, I had to find my education about that part of life elsewhere.

Masturbation was another unspoken word. At the time, I did not know the word even existed. Any healthy child would be curious about their genitals, especially when they feel good to the touch. But when I learned that it was "bad," I felt like I was doing something *extremely* wrong. I felt so guilty, even to the point that I did not think I would be able to have children. In my mind, touching myself was wrong and bad — a great way to contextualize my sexuality. Boy, was I confused.

Also, neither Mom nor Dad (heaven forbid), ever talked about menstruation. Fortunately, I received a little sex education from my Girl Scout Troop leaders. I went to my sister, Betty, when my period started and she helped me. I was too embarrassed to talk with my Mother about it since she had never mentioned the subject. At least, I do not remember her doing so.

"Good girls do not make-out; they will get a bad reputation." was the main message I received from my family and my church. For the most part, I was to be prim and proper in my relationships with boys. That notion definitely kept me out of trouble! I remember my older brother, Joe, telling me to never have sex until I was married. Fortunately, a more positive message that I received from the church was that sexuality is "a gift from God." That positive statement was very important for me to hear, and I felt a sense of calmness.

In my first attempts to have children, I struggled with infertility. All four of our children were helped along with fertility medicine. I cannot help but wonder how the shame, negativity, and guilt surrounding the issue of my sexuality might have contributed to the infertility problems I had. I also wonder how that negativity contributed to a whole host of other psychological problems I faced as an adult.

~

I lacked understanding about sex and sexuality and I also lacked confidence in academics. School was tough for me. I started the first grade when I was five years old and struggled to keep up with my classmates my entire school-aged life. Kindergarten did not exist back then. I know I had a learning disability which is now referred to as an alternative learning style. Because I had to struggle so hard and so long, I grew up thinking I was stupid. My self-esteem and self-confidence were damaged in a big way.

Athletics saved me to a large degree. The sports arena is where I experienced the successes which I so desperately needed. In elementary school, I would always win blue ribbons at field day, and I really do mean *always*. The 100-yard dash, the 50-yard dash, the three-legged race, and the wheelbarrow race were usually won by me and/or my partners. All year long I looked so forward to field day – my favorite day of the school year.

In high school, I was an awesome tennis player and still am, no conceitedness intended! My big sister, Betty Blythe, helped me start my tennis career when I was nine years old. Anything she did, I did. At thirteen, I was the Nashville Interscholastic League (NIL) champion — what a mouthful to say. I was a freshman at Hillsboro High School in Nashville, and my opponent, Brannon was a senior at Cohn High School. The day before we were to play the championship match, she asked if I would hit some balls with her. I thought it was a good idea, so I accepted, thinking if I hit the ball really hard and looked really good, she might get nervous, and I would beat her and win the tournament.

The next day at school my tennis coach, yelled at me for playing with Brannon. She thought that it was a disadvantage to let my opponent see how I played. I had never seen her so angry.

Well, to make a long story short, my strategy worked. To my surprise and everyone else's, I won. I, scrawny little, Carolyn Dianne Lackey, the academic runt of Hillsboro High, was the NIL Tennis Champion, thank-you-very-much. I may not have known much about math, science, sex, or menstruation, but I could play on the tennis court. In order for me to play on the tennis team for the next three years, I had to keep my grades up, and boy did I struggle.

My academic progress inched along, but in athletics, I bounded. At the beginning of my senior year, I and another classmate were elected alternate cheerleaders. I had tried out every year and finally made the squad. Almost every six weeks, one of the freshman cheerleaders did not make the required grade point average that she needed to be able to cheer. Since I could identify with her struggle, I felt bad for her. It could have easily been me. So, every other game, I got to cheer in her place. I was so happy and had a blast. I could do a forward flip and turn multiple cartwheels, which most of the cheerleaders could not do. All to be classified under 'hot stuff.'

At the end of my senior year, my Hillsboro classmates voted for me to have two superlatives, Friendliest and Most School Spirit. I was and still am very humbled to this day. The words written by classmates in my 1961 senior annual put me to my knees. I recently sat down and finally took the time to read all of their kind thoughts about me. My self-worth soared. Thanks to all!

Kenny Hoffman and Dianne Lackey
Best School Spirit
Hillsboro High School, 1961

As for college, I continued to struggle academically and excel in athletics. I only made one 'A' in my first quarter at the University of Tennessee, Knoxville, and it was in weightlifting. The rest were Ds.

Another saving grace for me was music. I was at the University of Tennessee in Knoxville, TN for one year and decided to return to Nashville to attend Peabody College for

Teachers. While in school, I took voice lessons and hoped to perform solo and/or join a band. I love music, especially singing.

My dream actually came true. Two guys from Vanderbilt asked me to sing in a folk music trio similar to Peter, Paul, and Mary, but we were Chip, Jimmy, and Dianne and called ourselves The Cape Gay Trio. The name came about by spinning a globe while Jimmy's finger was on it. When the globe stopped spinning, his finger landed on Cape Gay. Hence, The Cape Gay Trio was born — brilliant!

Jimmy was also the leader of a rock and roll combo called The Wild Hots at Vanderbilt. He asked me if I would be interested in singing with the group. I thought I had died and gone to heaven. I sang in a gig with them at the Phi Delta Theta fraternity house one Saturday night, and the rest was history. I became the female vocalist with The Wild Hots! My musical instruments were the maracas, the tambourine, and the cowbell. We played just about every weekend at sorority and fraternity parties and Nashville social events, etc. Because it was a more traditional time, and I was a woman amongst men, the band decided that for my safety one of them should pick me up and take me home after each gig. I thought it was a nice gesture and one that I appreciated. They called it "Lackey Duty." They took turns chauffeuring me, but occasionally one of them would forget it was their night for "Lackey Duty" and would accidentally invite a date. This circumstance created somewhat of a problem. It was uncouth to have a date in the front seat and your female bandmate in the back and, God forbid, your female bandmate in the front seat and your date in the back! At the last minute, whoever it was that forgot would try to find a sub, so I became a pain in the ass to the rest of the band. This I did not appreciate.

4

My Buddy

I picked up on the fact that Buddy Benedict, our drummer, started frequenting the "Lackey Duty" responsibility. He was Jimmy's sub one night, then Tommy's sub the next night, and Rod's the next. These "accidental" dates slowly became actual dates. Not long after, we were considered "going steady," and Buddy gave me his fraternity pin. In those days, that was the protocol in college prior to being engaged to be married. A few months later, he asked me to marry him. I said, "Yes," and he presented me with his Grandmother's beautiful diamond engagement wedding ring.

We were engaged for about a year and then married. Buddy says, "I was assigned Lackey Duty two or three times in a row, and now I have it for the rest of my life!" We married during my junior year at Peabody College and his senior year at Vanderbilt on June 23, 1964.

The Wild Hots, 1963
Left to right: Rod Daniel, Jimmy Hunt, Tom Wells, Buddy, and I

Prior to Buddy's and my marriage, there were a couple of issues that I needed to discuss with him. For one, Uncle Lunsford, my Dad's brother, had schizophrenia. I thought there was a chance Buddy might not want to continue dating me if he knew mental illness was in my family. To his family, lineage was very important and as a result, they were pretty "gene-conscious." There was a Senior Andrew Benedict, a Junior, a Third (Buddy) and before that, many others. That being said, I didn't want to wait any longer to let the cat out of the bag. I was overly sensitive about this subject, but after I told Buddy, he was not concerned. It was a relief for me because that issue was something I had always been insecure about in terms of marriage and having children. After we talked, I felt reassured, calmer, and that I could relax into the relationship.

Next topic of discussion – dinner. I wanted to let Buddy know that it was very important to me, especially when we have children, that in the evening, we would eat together as a family. This may seem strange and even trivial, but this is something that my Dad rarely did, and I wanted my marriage with Buddy to be different, I wanted it to last. I distinctly remember one night when I was in high school, my Dad came home late from work, and I had intentionally stayed up to talk with him. I begged him to start coming home to eat with us on a regular basis as a family. I cried, and for a while, he tried, but it was short-lived. Things went back to the same old same old. I was angry, but at least I got my feelings off my chest.

Well, after these issues were out in the open, and Buddy agreed to come home for dinner, it wasn't long before we got married. I was determined, almost to the point of being obsessive, that our marriage and our love for each other were going to last. Since my parent's marriage ended in divorce, I was anxious to prevent another dysfunctional relationship in our future family. The cycle had to be broken, and I knew Buddy and I could find a way to break it.

A few months into our marriage, I read about a communication workshop being held in Atlanta by a guy named Curry Overton. "Relational Communication," was the title of the event. The more I read about its content, the more I knew it was crucial for Buddy and me to attend. I explained to him what the workshop was about and expressed my desire for us to go. Being the polite newlywed that he was, he agreed, but I could tell that he was very reluctant.

When we arrived in Atlanta on a Friday night, we walked into a candlelit room with the other attendees sitting on bean bags in a circle. The look on Buddy's face said it all. I can't remember the last time he or I sat on a bean bag, let alone with other people, and lit candles. He was like a duck out of water, and I was like a duck in unfamiliar water, but willing to float.

After the lecture and discussion that night, we went back to our motel barely saying a word to each other. When we got in bed, quietness prevailed.

"We need to go home first thing in the morning," Buddy said.

My heart sank. I almost swallowed my tongue. I was expecting his disapproval, but not to that extent. I lay real still looking at the ceiling and grasping for a response. I had really enjoyed the evening, except for his stiffness, and I wanted to stay for the entire weekend. I could tell that Currey Overton knew what he was talking about and that the information he could provide was invaluable.

Trying to be calm, I finally found words. I told Buddy that he could go back home, but I was going to stay put, and that he could pick me up at the Greyhound station on Sunday.

He didn't like this plan, and I knew he wouldn't. This is the guy who picked me up and took me home from band practice so that I would be safe. He wasn't about to agree to me taking a five-hour Greyhound bus ride alone from Atlanta.

I told him I wasn't going to leave without at least giving it a chance and, aside from that, we can't get our money back so what is there to lose?

During that first night on beanbags, interestingly enough, we talked with our group about the importance of compromise in a relationship. So, putting this recently acquired concept to use, I came up with another idea.

I suggested that we give it a try one more day. I proposed that instead of staying all day Saturday and Sunday, we could drive home first thing Sunday morning. I said all this while hoping that he would loosen up on Saturday and be willing, and even better, wanting, to stay the entire time.

Saturday went great, and we learned a lot. Bright and early on Sunday morning, Buddy was packed and more than ready to go home. I was disappointed, but we had made a deal, and that was that. We are still married after fifty-seven years, so they must not have said anything on Sunday that we didn't know already, or could not figure out.

Sometime later that year, we attended a beanbag-free, marriage enrichment weekend sponsored by our church. Antoinette and Leon Smith, one of the couples who started the entire marriage enrichment movement, were our facilitators. They were a godsend to our marriage. They invited Buddy and me to help them on some of their retreats and basically trained us to be facilitators. When Buddy graduated from Vanderbilt Divinity School in 1983, he was assigned to be the associate minister to our church, West End United Methodist. Marriage enrichment became one of his/ our responsibilities. I came along for free.

That isn't to say things were happily-ever-after from there. There was a point where Buddy's and my marriage came real close to falling apart, and I think mainly due to my low self-worth. Granted, Buddy had his faults too, but I think my state of mind was the main problem. I was blaming him for everything under the sun. I was extremely jealous and did not trust him. I could not get along very well with my in-laws, but now I recognize that wasn't totally my fault. I felt extremely self-conscious at parties and usually did not have a very good time. I was basically an insecure and unhappy camper on the inside, appearing to have it all together on the outside.

What I never wanted to happen seemed exactly what was happening, and I did not seem to have any control over making things different. Divorce, one of my greatest fears, was looking like it might be a reality. I was scared to death. In the course of one or two years, I sought out help from two of our ministers, a psychologist, a psychiatrist, a social worker, and friends. Along with the fear of divorce was the equally frightening fear that I was going "crazy" due to my genetic relationship with schizophrenia.

Buddy was a student at the Vanderbilt Divinity School, and a part of his training was to have sessions with a psychologist. He asked me if I wanted to go with him. I agreed, hoping that help was on the way. Progress seemed slow. The psychologist mostly listened, and we did most of the talking. At least, we were talking in the presence of an objective and trained psychologist. Our therapy sessions ended just before Buddy's graduation. Some progress in our relationship was accomplished, but definitely not enough. Thankfully we found a new therapist not long after that.

5

A Big Change

About three years after our marriage, the worst happened. Schizophrenia re-entered our family through my brother, Donald. Don is four years younger than I. It wasn't like something unfamiliar or unrecognizable had entered him, instead, it was like he had died, and we were in mourning. As a child, he was so fun-loving and playful, now he was withdrawn and could not carry on a conversation. He was attending the University of Tennessee in Knoxville and had to come home. Needless to say, our whole family was absolutely devastated.

When this happened all of the dysfunction in my family was brought to a head. Our greatest fear was happening right before our eyes. Who will be next? Will it be me? What are we going to do with Donald? Did I do something to contribute to his illness? How did I treat him when we were little? — these were some of the questions that popped up in our minds. I vividly remembered scaring him by chasing him around our yard with a dead mouse. At that point, I didn't know much about schizophrenia and naively thought I had something to do with his problem. Doctors reassured me that was not the case.

Our oldest sister, Betty Blythe, helped Mom and Dad decide a plan of action with psychiatrists and counselors at the Vanderbilt University Psychiatric Hospital. Dad and Mom blamed themselves. Some of our family members went to the Dee Dee Wallace Mental Health Center in Nashville for family counseling. Usually, Mom, Betty Blythe, Fran, Donald, and I attended the sessions. Other members of our family could not handle going to family therapy for one reason or another. It was understandable, he was one of us, and in a sense, it was as if we all were diagnosed together. We felt so vulnerable and helpless.

Donald and our youngest brother, Thomas, were very close growing up. Tom idolized Donald. Don taught Tom how to drive; they were in the same high school fraternity; they fished together; played tennis and baseball together; you name it, they did it together. After college, and after Don's diagnosis, Tom moved to California to pursue his dream in the movie industry. He established a film and commercial locations production company that still thrives today. I can't help but think his move was, in part, an escape from the intensity, the pain, and the agonizing reality that his big brother and best friend had disappeared into thin air. Tom got as far away as he could, and I understand. Those of us who stayed at home had the painful duty of seeing it up-close, going to visit Donald in the psychiatric ward, and trying to make some sense of it all. It was very sad and stressful.

Big sister, Betty Blythe took the bull by the horns and started researching places that would be best for him. She was married and had moved to Washington, D.C. with her husband, Jesse. After they moved, she became a member of the National Schizophrenic Association which gave her access to the names of hospitals and residential care centers all over the country. She and our family's main goal was to find a setting where Donald would not be locked up in a mental institution like our Uncle Lunsford was for years. Donald's anger about what was happening to him was evident. I cannot imagine how difficult it would be to accept this state of mind at such an early age. I would be mad as hell.

Donald was an in-patient resident at the Vanderbilt Hospital in Nashville for a while and then, at Betty's suggestion, went to the Sheppard and Enoch Pratt Hospital in Towson, Maryland. It was relatively close to Virginia where Betty and her husband, Jesse, had recently moved. She could keep a better watch over Don's progress there. Donald was in a psychiatric ward against his will and did not like it. One day he ran away, and no one could find him. He showed up later that night at Betty and Jesse's doorstep, fifty-two miles away, in Falls Church, Virginia. After that incident, he lived with them for six months. Weekly, Betty would take him to the hospital that he escaped from for out-patient therapy. Betty was working on Senator Edmund Muskie's political campaign and Don, having out-patient treatment, was able to take on a job in the campaign under her supervision.

What a sister and brother-in-law Betty and Jesse were! Their love and dedication to Donald and our family can never be measured in value – *phenomenal* is all I can say. I am sitting here typing and looking out my window, taking deep breaths and thinking about how overwhelming all this was and still is. I especially think about Betty and Jesse and all they must have gone through while Donald lived with them for six months. Betty told me that Jesse never complained. Unbelievable! Again, all I can say is, thank you, Betty and Jesse!

In Betty's relentless research for a "non-locked" facility, she found a residential care center called, Rancho Verde in San Jose, California. There were restrictions there, but, being locked up all day was not one of them, thank God. Donald liked Rancho Verde for the most part and even made some friends and a girlfriend that he would tell us about. Don remained there for three or four years, and one day called us saying he wanted to come back to Nashville. I couldn't wrap my mind around how that was possible.

At that time Buddy's and my oldest daughter, Beth was six and our twins, Andy and Fran, were three. Needless to say, I could not help very much in Donald's transition and care. So, Betty, Mom, Dad, brother John, and sister, Fran, along with the Vanderbilt Psychiatric staff, came up with this plan of action — outpatient therapy, once a week, while living at home with Mom, Dad, John, and Fran. What an ordeal it was.

Our family was living on pins and needles. It was difficult because Don needed to be watched all the time. His actions were unpredictable. Betty continued her quest to find unlocked facilities. She knew first hand that the above plan of action would not last very long. By the way, in those days, she did not have the luxury of receiving help from a computer or a cell phone. After two anxiety-filled months, Betty called and said that the Anne Sippi Clinic, an unlocked residential care center for adults with schizophrenia in Alhambra, California, had an opening for a new resident. Donald said he wanted to give the facility a try. He remained there a number of years until the clinic made the decision to no longer house long-term residents. Even though the last attempt to move him back to Nashville was hard and grueling, we wanted to give it another try and so did Donald.

The move to Nashville was inevitable, but this time we were determined to make it work. A psychiatrist at Johns Hopkins University had developed a plan for an in-patient community mental health center in Maryland. Betty and Fran were inspired by his model and started looking into real estate around the Nashville area. Our Lackey family chose a beautiful thirty-acre farm, with a nice farmhouse on the property, located in Franklin, Tennessee. Betty and Fran named the facility, The Center for Living and Learning. It was going to be a place where adults with schizophrenia could live in an unlocked facility, receive treatment, and learn the social and technical skills to find a job. It was a place that would not only give residents the opportunity to live comfortably but also allow them to plan for the future, with the aim of living a more independent life.

Don was home for good this time. He and an attendant were our first residents. As of now, he has lived there for thirty years. He loves his farm and shares it with twenty-five other residents. My sister, Fran is the CEO. She has a dedicated around the clock staff and a board of directors. Her husband, Scooter Clippard, is her non-paid assistant, project manager, and chief fundraiser. Annually, Scooter heads up our major fundraising golf tournament. Unselfishly, he volunteered his time the day we decided to make "The Center" a reality. Currently, it has an organic CSA (Community Supported Agriculture) program, music, art, yoga and pottery classes, pickleball, tennis, four state-of-the-art homes, two horses, two dogs (Kei and Stella), and we take annual trips to the beach and mountains.

It was a long road, but we did it — "Uncle Donald has a farm (and a home), E-I, E-I, O!!!!

Before our parents died, they requested that all of us siblings take good care of Donald for as long as he lives. Needless to say, we are fulfilling their request. Our unanimous response to that is, "He ain't heavy; he's our brother."

Due to the archaic, sedative drugs Donald was given early on, he developed a condition called tardive dyskinesia, a muscular disorder resulting from psychotropic drugs

(Thorazine, Haldol, and Prolixin) prescribed in the '40s, '50s, and even early '60s. Tardive dyskinesia caused Don's muscles to turn into knots, and his limbs to contort in pain. These drugs were used for sedation purposes only. They had no brain-healing qualities and the risk of detrimental negative side-effects was high. Today, these drugs of the past are considered first-generation drugs. Fortunately and miraculously, we now have second-generation drugs. These drugs actually do something to help the brain function normally. Dopamine, Serotonin, Norepinephrine, and Glutamate, which are natural chemicals in our brains, function much more effectively while using the miracle drug, Clozaril (generic is Clozapine). Hallucinations have been eliminated to a large extent because of this drug. No one thought that tardive dyskinesia could be reversed but, Clozaril and second-generation drugs, along with physical therapy, physical work, and vitamins have enabled Donald to accomplish this reversal.

Before Donald started taking Clozaril, Dr. William Petrie, head of the Psychiatric Department at the Vanderbilt Medical Center, requested that Don be approved as a "trial study patient" for the drug. He went over all the risks involved with Donald, Mom, and Fran. Fran told me that she thought it was impossible for Donald to understand all that was going on. She said he had been incoherent all day and the idea of him making a rational decision about treatment risks and methods seemed next to impossible. On top of that, his muscular condition made it difficult for him to physically sign a waiver.

To everyone's surprise, Donald walked over to Dr. Petrie and clearly said, "Dr. Petrie, I will do anything to get out of this hellish nightmare I'm living in." Fran said that he was so lucid at that moment and effortlessly and accurately signed his name, Donald Enoch Lackey, on the dotted line. It was a miracle. Before that day, he would sign his name as, "Santa Claus" or "Ichabod Crane."

In 1987, Don went on Clozaril as a "trial study patient," before the F.D.A. approved it in the United States. It has been the most effective drug Don has taken in twenty-eight years. Being in close quarters on a daily basis with patients who take this drug, and seeing their progress, Fran says, "Clozaril helps people get their brain back. Right now, there is no complete cure for schizophrenia, but a cure is on the way. The key to finding a cure is sticking with it."

6

News Nobody Wanted to Hear

1. "Dad, I'm under my desk hiding from someone shooting a gun. Dad, I'm so scared."

On April 20, 1999, I was eating lunch at home and turned on CNN. This statement was being aired live as a man listened to a cell phone call from his son at the Columbine High School in Columbine, Colorado. Oh my God, I could not believe what I was hearing. This boy and his father were experiencing total terror, and it felt as if I were right there under that desk experiencing it with them. I do not know if the boy survived that terrible and horrific day. I pray that he did.

2. A fourteen-year-old boy in Paducah, Kentucky, opened fire on a group of his peers who were attending an early

morning prayer service around the flagpole at their high school.

3. A thirty-seven-year-old Dad in Shelbyville, Tennessee shot and killed his four children out of anger with their Mother, his ex-wife. I do not recall the date of this event or the one before in Paducah, but they happened before 9/11 in 2001.

4. Three rabbis were brutally murdered in Jerusalem.

5. A class of innocent kindergarten children was gunned down by a young man at Sandy Hook Elementary School in Newtown, Conneticut.

6. Persons attending a movie in Aurora, Colorado near Denver, were shot down by another young man.

7. NEWS FLASH — November 13, 2013 — State of Emergency, Paris, France — 129 people dead and 350+ injured — determined to be an ISIS attack. It is 7:00 p.m. here in Nashville and 2:00 a.m. in Paris. Anderson Cooper on CNN is announcing that the attacks were occurring in multiple locations — a soccer stadium, bars, restaurants, and a theatre while hostages lying on the floor were being shot by gunmen.

As I grieve with our fellow human beings in Paris, both victims and perpetrators, these thoughts arise: In the case of ISIS terrorists, we are dealing with persons who, over the years, for one reason or another, have afflicted themselves with severe low self-worth, mental self-pity, and self-hate. These hate-filled choices have lead to chronic mental distortions, mental illness, and radicalization. The terrorists have chosen to reverse their mental torture from within to without by inflicting it on innocent fellow human beings and using military-style AK47s to massacre their victims.

A witness at the Paris theatre said, "We were being shot at like birds."

On some sick, irrational, thwarted subconscious or conscious level, these individuals have deduced that their actions are right and justified. This is the epitome of true evil.

8. NEWS FLASH — October 1, 2015 — Oregon shooting at a Community College – 10 killed. President Obama expresses his anger at the lack of gun control and ongoing gun violence. The gunman had 6 guns with him, and 7 were found at a motel room where he lived with his Mother. His shocked Dad lives in California. On a national news report, mental illness surfaces as a possible cause.

When are we going to connect the dots? How was this young man treated when he was a child or even before birth when he was in the womb? I will never believe that he was born into this world destined and/or wanting to kill innocent people. Hopefully, he came into this world as a healthy and innocent child — a child with no fears, no drugs, or hang-ups. Many questions about his background need to be asked and answered. Before birth, were his parents smokers, heavy alcohol users, drug abusers? Were one or both of his parents or relatives sexual abusers? Was he emotionally or physically abused? All of these questions need to be asked. Ideally, he would enter into a family with a clean and healthy slate to work with as he matures. Unfortunately and sadly, I'm sure this was not the case for him and so many others. And this is a noticeable pattern over the last ten to twenty years.

Many young children are sexually abused and mistreated by parents, teachers, relatives, or other uninformed and uneducated adults who have been treated the same way when they were vulnerable children. Their self-worth, self-esteem, and dignity have been severely damaged. This devastating cycle, if not broken, will continue to be repeated over and over again. What are we going to do about this?

What earth-shattering intervention is going to break these horrendous outcomes? We are in the middle of a global psychological crisis. White Supremacists, Al-Qaeda, and ISIS gangs are three examples of groups founded on deep-seated hatred that have existed for many decades. How long will Palestinians and Israelis continue their obsessive fighting? All of these examples have roots related to chronic distortions of the mind that have not been and are not being dealt with. Where and how does healing begin in all of the above?

9. NEWS FLASH — October 6, 2015 — CNN and FACEBOOK NEWSFEED. An eleven-year-old boy accused of murdering an eight-year-old girl who would not share her puppy with him. He shot her with a gun that he found in his home.

Anderson Cooper did a special report on this horrendous incident. He said that the boy would be tried as an adult or as a juvenile under Tennessee laws. The judge would have to decide.

I have an eleven-year-old Grandson, and I cannot conceive of him taking a gun and shooting another child because he or she would not share their pet. The young girl, victim #1, is dead and will no longer live her life, and her family is absolutely devastated. The young boy, victim #2, is alive. Yes, I say victim because he most likely is a victim of his distorted environmental circumstances. Most perpetrators, such as he, usually kill themselves after killing their victim. But, he is not old enough to realize the degree of the consequences that he will have to face. Now, the young boy will be taken out of his home.

What was going on or not going on in his home? His anger was obviously out of control and he took out his anger on this innocent little girl. Was his family oblivious to the degree of his anger? What about his pediatrician, teachers, relatives, and therapists? Did someone not observe abnormalcy in his behavior? I imagine there were red flags flying.

The really sad thing to me is that most, if not all, of the above, could have been prevented with psychological therapeutic intervention chosen by mature adults in his life. Getting to the roots of the mental distortions that developed over his eleven little years was imperative. If in fact, he lived in a neglectful environment, it's too bad that it took killing

48

another person to remove him from it. Hopefully, he will be given another chance and get the therapy he needs. In my opinion, he is worthy and able to be healed.

10. NEWS FLASH — December 25, 2020 — On Christmas morning, a sixty-three-year-old male left his Nashville residence and drove an RV to the downtown historic area on 2nd Avenue North. He parked in front of the AT&T building, which houses the transmission equipment for multiple states, and after fifteen minutes his vehicle exploded. The suicide bomber was the only fatality. Many storefront buildings were damaged, and internet and cell phone services were interrupted for three days.

7

Keeping Life Balanced

From these past and now present experiences I started connecting some very important dots. It is like the pieces to a puzzle are starting to fit together to form a larger picture. The answers to my own questions are becoming evident. Questions such as – why is this increased violence happening? Why are so many young men resorting to gunning down and killing people, even little children? What happened to these young people, in their childhood, that created such hatred for themselves and others? Why would a father kill members of his own family? Why 9/11? Why is ISIS evolving and dominating? Why war? When and how is all this evil going to stop?

Most of us are aware of the mind-body-spirit approach to life — that a full experience of self and the world involves an intricate conversation between our mind, our body, and our spirit. I have gained a lot from adopting this mindset and have applied it to how I live my life.

I have found it important to pay attention not only to these aspects of my being but also to the study of them. I practice looking inward while also listening to the people that have dedicated their lives to these fields. So if I were to rephrase the mind-body-spirit model I would talk about it in terms of considering the *study* of the mind, body, and spirit — the "ologies" — Psychology, Biology, and Theology.

Some people believe that science and religion have no business intertwining, but I disagree. There are two books that have helped me bridge the gap between these fields — *The Road Less Traveled* by M. Scott Peck and *I'm O.K. You're O.K.* by Thomas A. Harris, M.D. These two books have shown me that when science and religion work in unison, their impact strengthens.

The road that Dr. Scott Peck is referring to in *The Road Less Traveled* is the road of "dynamic psychotherapy." Dynamic means "ongoing" and "psychotherapy" is the process of healing the mind. So, in order for "ongoing healing of the mind" to occur, the client and their clinical therapist examine the client's past and present. By the client's understanding of how both positive and negative experiences have modified their brain, changes in thinking can begin to occur. With this new understanding, the person in therapy is enabled to modify their behavior. Once understood, this experience is never forgotten. This process is not a quick and easy psychological "fix." From birth, it has taken time for all of us to get into the states of mind we find ourselves in. So, consequently, it will take time to get ourselves out of the states of mind we feel are holding us back for one reason or another. Most people will not choose this "road less traveled" because it takes time, effort, and honesty about oneself in the presence of a well-trained, objective third party. Unfortunately, this road of well-being is less traveled for many reasons. First of all, who wants to be vulnerable and air their dirty laundry with anyone, much less a therapist? The stigmas associated with mental health and mental illness freak out many people. In addition, the thought sometimes prevails that if one goes to a therapist, he or she will appear to be weak and cannot handle their situation or life on their own. Who wants to be exposed? Why do we think we need to be so strong on our own? Are we deceiving ourselves?

The second book, *I'm O.K. You're O.K.*, written by Thomas A. Harris, M.D, is about Transactional Analysis. So, what is that? Dr. Harris uses an egg to illustrate his premise. We all start out as a healthy fertilized egg that is close to or is, perfect. He is talking about the literal fertilized egg when we are conceived in the womb. He then uses the metaphor of an egg with a shell to describe how our lives evolve. According to Dr. Harris, we are born into a world of positive and negative environmental experiences. Cracks, mainly associated with negative life experiences, begin to appear in the egg. As we mature more and more of these cracks appear. These negative cracks begin to affect our sense of self-worth, self-confidence, and self-esteem. We all have these negative experiences to one degree or another. So, can we heal or patch our egg? Dr. Harris suggests that we can with Dynamic Psychotherapy.

And once we really understand why we are functioning as we are, we become more in control of our issues as opposed to our issues being in control of us. Once our sense of control shifts, our confidence and/or self-worth increase, and the process of patching or healing our egg begins.

All of us have a choice to make. Do we fall into the "stigma trap" mentioned above in regard to our fears around therapy and ignore our issues? Or do we go by our gut and not be controlled by our fears and/or what people might think if we have a "shrink"? (By the way, I do not like that often used word.)

At the fast pace our society is going, the easiest and most tempting choice is to ignore the choice. I have tried both — ignoring and confronting — and have found that taking the time to understand my issues, with the help of an objective and well-trained therapist, is the way to go. In doing so, I have been enabled to take giant steps rather than baby steps in my ongoing quest for wholeness. Everyone will not choose this route, but it has worked for me in unbelievable ways.

One of the last things I thought I would ever do was write a book. Before, and in the early years of my dynamic psychotherapy, I was basically insecure and unsure of myself and my abilities. Thirteen years ago, I told my psychotherapist, Dr. Ted Morton, "I want to write a book about all these things that are happening to me, but I do not think I can do it." He said, "You are not ready to do it yet," insinuating that I could and would do it later in my life if I wanted to. Well, he was right. Now, I have an insatiable desire to share my successes and struggles. At the time, he had much more confidence in me than I had in myself. He was and still is, a master. All my "cracks" are not completely healed, and I am not a perfect specimen *yet*, but I know I can be of help to a lot of people by sharing where I am in my life journey, and how I got here. So, that is why I write. I am a person who knows life is good, most of the time, and wants to know and share that goodness to the extent that is possible in this lifetime. I have worked hard to achieve mental, physical, and spiritual balance. Maintaining this balance is an ongoing pursuit.

~

As I have mentioned before, in my experience, the major areas of study for this balance are Psychology, Biology, and Theology. Each of these three "ologies," or disciplines, needs to be separate but mutually functioning and inclusive of the other for balance, wholeness, and wellness. Let's take them one at a time.

The following diagrams are my attempt to make my abstract and conceptual thinking visual and understandable. The entire structure — a globe, circle, or ball — is representative of the total person or soul surrounded by God's love. I am using the word, "God," but, Higher Power, Force, Holy Spirit, Energy Source, or whatever terminology you associate with a power that is greater than yourself, can be used.

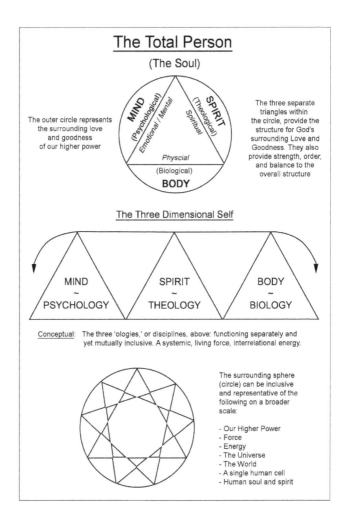

The Total Person
(The Soul)

MIND
(Psychological)
Emotional / Mental

SPIRIT
(Theological)
Spiritual

Physcial
(Biological)
BODY

The outer circle represents
the surrounding love
and goodness
of our higher power

The three separate
triangles within
the circle, provide the
structure for God's
surrounding Love and
Goodness. They also
provide strength, order,
and balance to the
overall structure

The Three Dimensional Self

MIND
~
PSYCHOLOGY

SPIRIT
~
THEOLOGY

BODY
~
BIOLOGY

Conceptual: The three 'ologies,' or disciplines, above: functioning separately and
yet mutually inclusive. A systemic, living force, interrelational energy.

The surrounding sphere
(circle) can be inclusive
and representative of the
following on a broader
scale:

- Our Higher Power
- Force
- Energy
- The Universe
- The World
- A single human cell
- Human soul and spirit

In the first diagram, the three triangles are stacked and appear to be one within the circle. The three "ologies" — Psychology, Theology, and Biology — come together in unison, yet are separate from each other. These disciplines provide the structure for God's love. When working together they create wholeness and/or transformation that is attainable with ongoing intentionality by the individual person.

In the second diagram, picture a clothesline with three equilateral triangles hanging from it. Imagine, taking the line at each end with your fingers, and making a circle as the ends meet.

In the third diagram, I envision this cylindrical structure as a three-dimensional, all-inclusive, active, and viable globe, which creates balance, wholeness, and wellness in our world and our universe. The circle can represent a single cell within all living things, containing the same internal "ologies" supporting the structure of the cell. The three "ologies" need to be given top priority as we live our lives. Since we are all unique individuals, our experiences will be different as we develop, but I think our goals of balance, wellbeing, and wholeness are common to all of us. They are seemingly universal and achievable. The networking or fabric of inherent goodness and wholeness can develop, depending on our life choices and experiences as we grow and mature. Below, I will share how this concept is working for me in more tangible and practical ways.

Theology – Spirit

Spiritual Development

I will begin with the discipline of Theology. Theology is defined as the study of (ology) God (Theo). So, how do I study God? This morning, as I do many mornings, I awoke pretty much in a fog, feeling loose ended to some degree in my head. I fixed my usual coffee and healthy cereal bowl which consists of raw oatmeal, seasonal fruits, and various seeds (pumpkin, almonds, chia, hemp hearts, etc.) and milk. My husband, Buddy, Fran, our Nutritionist daughter, and I went outside to the tree swing in our front yard to enjoy our healthy and relaxed breakfast. After breakfast, my mind started to become more lucid and focused.

To begin the day early and not so "me" centered, we read from three sources – The Inclusive Bible (The First Egalitarian Translation-meaning sex-inclusive), *Disciplines,* a daily ecumenical (meaning all denominations included) devotional book published by The Upper Room in Nashville, and another daily devotional book, *Jesus Calling: Enjoying Peace In His Presence,* by Sara Young. Recently we've added Angela Howell's book entitled *Finding the Gift: Daily Meditations for Mindfulness.* Our daughter, Elysabeth is a craniosacral therapist and leads a meditation class incorporating Qigong which I attend every other week. I list these resources that are personal to me and Buddy. Your choices may be different depending on the uniqueness of your faith — Muslim, Jewish, Hindu, Buddhist, etc. The point is a daily routine, a priority of touching base with a Higher Power that is greater than yourself. This may seem awkward at first. You may not be able to get to it every morning, but that is fine, no pressure. Just be aware that the ultimate goal is to try to "touch base" daily and make it a priority. The devotional guides I have chosen are brief and take no longer than fifteen minutes to read through. For me, it is important that the amount of time I spend doing a devotional is workable with my daily schedule. I am sure you feel the same way with the many responsibilities you have.

In addition to daily devotions, Buddy and I attend a Sunday School class and a worship service regularly. These two rituals provide small group discussions and community worship. We do not attend every Sunday, but most. The goal is to be as regular as possible. Again, no pressure; however, I have found that community and worship consistency is important. Currently, during the COVID-19 Pandemic, we are "Zooming" into the online worship service and Sunday school class.

Spiritual development is a priority for me. Studying the Bible under the direction of well-educated, inclusive, and grounded Biblical theologians is very important. When choosing a place of worship, the minister is key. His or her theological training needs to be of utmost consideration. The senior or head minister usually teaches a weekly Bible Study. I chose to attend these classes in addition to being a member of a weekly smaller discussion group where we focus on a topic or book to discuss. I believe it is especially important to follow a broader and encompassing faith, one that is mainstream and historically represents its faith in a contemporary context. I do not believe in spiritual extremism. The Religious Right Movement bothers me. I do not believe Jesus is the only way, nor do I believe that the Bible should be read literally. As far as I am concerned, those advocating a religion without respect for the inclusiveness of other faiths are condescending and shortsighted.

The Struggle

I have noticed a migration away from an organized spiritual belief system, especially in younger generations. Many Millennials seem to be removing themselves from Christianity and other faiths and not considering them as spiritual options. Frankly, I don't blame them, but it makes me sad. Far-right religious groups have done an extreme injustice and disservice to Christian communities and organized faiths in general. As far as Christianity is concerned, I believe we are "throwing the baby (Jesus) out with the bathwater" when we consider Jesus to be the only way. Yes, he was and is very important in Christianity and other religions as well, but he is not a replacement for our Higher Power. In my opinion, extremely conservative religious groups are trying to make an idol out of Jesus. I believe Jesus would be outraged by this approach.

I have found that other examples of religious extremism can be seen in faith groups who adhere to the literal interpretation of the Bible. Some church congregations read the Bible word for word, as the inerrant word of God without understanding the historical background from which the text is written. A good example of this is using "the devil" as a personified evil who is hiding, lurking, and creating bad things for people. Historically, this misconception developed from a religious group of people called Zoroastrians, who, for their lack of understanding and fear of "evil spirits" personified sin and evil and called it "the devil." It is a shame that some religions continue to instill this false fear into our current and future generations.

Instead of looking within ourselves to find many of the causes for our human struggles, blaming a "devil," others, or even God, can be a convenient and easy escape from dealing with our bad choices. By doing this, a person does not take responsibility for those choices and definitely does not get to the root of them. If we do not name the real source, the cycle is repeated over and over again, and change does not occur.

"God, why are you letting this happen to me?" and, "The devil made me do it," are thoughts that are forms of escape and denial.

In the past, I naively thought attending a mainstream, well-balanced church would provide me and my family with a supportive community that valued positive spiritual development. For a while the church did. In hindsight, I was totally unaware of a negative undercurrent that was developing in my community and in communities around the world. At this moment in time, a mainstream, well-balanced church is hard to come by. The church that I am attending is mixed with conservative and liberal members. For me, this is not an easy place to be. Why? A phenomenon that seems to exist is that conflicting beliefs in politics and religion have created a breakdown in communication. I get the sense that crossing the divide between church and state is unspeakable and as a result, discussions about controversial issues are rarely happening. It seems like the church is at a standstill. Currently, in my denomination (United Methodist), the members are divided over the LGBTQ issue. This is a repeat of the sixties segregation conflict. Some are accepting of the LGBTQ community, and some are not. I believe the division needs to happen if church members believe the LGBTQ community is "less than" for one biased reason or another. Due to my Christian upbringing, I still believe that the church is relevant. However, Christianity has gone astray. Change must occur in the direction that our Higher Power desires and I believe that change has to do with balance. The mind, body, and spirit need to be working together for our common good instead of operating separately and competing with each other.

In the sixties, major upheavals began to occur with segregation. When 9/11 happened, it was like the world woke up. Since then, radical transformations have been occurring. Multiple crises are happening all over the world. I believe that the COVID-19 Pandemic has brought these realizations into better focus. (Please refer to The Multiple Global Pandemics Tree drawing at the end of the book).

In many ways, our world seems to be in total chaos. Hopefully, before we all have nervous breakdowns trying to endure these extreme situations, major positive changes will begin to happen. I already see them happening, especially in regard to progress in the Black Lives Matter and LGBTQ movements. Peaceful protests are beginning to win out. I do not have the words to express my gratitude to CNN and their worldwide staff for doing the best that they can under extreme pressure and condemnation to bring about healing, change, and balance in our chaotic and unsettled world. I know that history will bear this out someday.

Struggle is a central theme of Theology. I believe one of the ways our human soul matures is through struggle. Struggling is important to a degree, but I do not think that we have to struggle as much and as hard as we do. So, why are we are struggling so much? What is missing? What are we doing wrong? We will always have some degree of struggle due to our, and other people's, inappropriate decisions. Those persons with whom we closely associate, such as family members and friends will make bad decisions that directly and indirectly cause us to struggle. Even decisions made by those whom we more distantly associate with — such as strangers and government officials — create struggle in our lives as well. It seems to me that since our Higher Power is helping us, we shouldn't have to struggle to the degree that we do. Maybe this is an incorrect assumption, but I do not think it is. I do not believe that our Higher Power has bestowed effortless goodness upon us. Instead, I believe that a Higher Power has given us an orderly system that we can work with to create goodness in our lives. For one reason or another, many are not choosing to plug into it.

Most of us, due to our negative past experiences, have unconsciously developed cluttered minds and a state of mental dis-ease or uncomfortableness. Consequently, our sense of self-worth and self-confidence have been altered in negative ways and as a result, the decisions we make can become distorted and possibly damaging to ourselves and others. Dis-ease in our minds can magnify our struggles to the point that they seem unbearable. We can become overwhelmed or even seemingly paralyzed at times.

The Holy

Faith is not a cure-all, but it is an important part of our well-being. More than anything, I believe that our Higher Power wants us to enjoy our lives on this earth. Our enjoyment of life is a prayer or response of thankfulness to God — appreciating nature, ourselves, and our relationships for example. Life is to be enjoyed, not all the time, but most of the time. The most amazing thing to me about living is that we can live pretty decent lives in spite of ourselves. Our Higher Power is trying to help us at every turn. Forgiveness is never-ending, and the inherent goodness and love of God are ever-present within and outside of ourselves. Are we able to see it, to feel it? Why or why not? Can we actually know the presence of the Holy? What, if anything, is standing in our way or better still, what are we *allowing* or even *choosing* to stand in our way? I think the answer to this question lies in taking responsibility in partnership with our Higher Power and working together with that power in the realms of our mind, body, and spirit for balance.

It is important to acknowledge the "holy" in our experiences. Why is this hard for us? If we so choose, I think we can be transformed by God's ever-present goodness and love. Can we help our Higher Power accomplish this? I think we can, but it takes intentionality on our part. We are not supposed to hand things over to God to do all the work. I'm talking about a working partnership with God. A quote comes to mind, "Let go, and let God." Another statement I often hear is, "Just pray and things will take care of themselves." Another is, "Everything happens for a reason." What or whose reason I ask?

In my opinion, if all the above statements are valid, we would be blatantly insulting the intelligence God gave us in the first place. These attitudes have not served us well in the past decades or even centuries. Taking responsibility for ourselves, in partnership with our Higher Power, is the first step. Removing ourselves from this partnership isn't the answer. "Let Go and Let God," in my opinion, is a copout.

God has given us incredible brains that enable us to maintain balance in our relationships with ourselves, others, and our Higher Power. A new approach will require us to use our grey matter on a deeper level and review ourselves. We must do this in order to have a healthy dependency on God versus an unhealthy one. We need to dig deeper!

It is easy to think that we must keep going forward to keep up with the fast pace of our technological world. Many might think they cannot afford to reflect. The truth is, we cannot afford not to reflect if we want to get our lives back on track. We have been off-track long enough. We are a busy society but, if true change is going to occur, it is essential that we take time to go back, to dig, and objectively review ourselves.

Let's take the bull by the horns and act *now* for ourselves and for future generations. Let's get a grip on the stigmas associated with mental health and/or mental illness that have created many unwarranted fears. These fears have suppressed our minds either consciously or subconsciously for generations. It's time for religion and science to stop competing with each other and start working together to recognize that both are God's gifts that can complement each other.

Psychology – Mind

I never thought anything good could come out of my brother, Donald being diagnosed with chronic schizophrenia. But mainly because of this traumatic event, Don, I, and other members of our family were fortunate enough to have the opportunity to develop psychologically, spiritually, and physically. I would even say, in these areas, we developed to a much greater and deeper degree than if he had remained well. However, his pain and ours will always remain with us on some level. In a very excruciating way, we all were forced to deal with mental illness head-on. We entered a whole new realm of deep thinking, which, in all honesty, we really did not want to do.

Our fears and inhibitions play tricks on us in our minds. Thoughts such as "I'm not worthy," "I don't deserve such and such," "Poor me," "Why me?", "I could've, would've, should've done this or that," "What will people think?" etc. These negative thoughts create a downward spiral of beating ourselves up and putting ourselves down. How exhausting is that? If not caught, we find ourselves in the throes of being overwhelmed, depressed, and sometimes seemingly mentally paralyzed. Why are we punishing ourselves? Why are we allowing these stigmas and distorted ways of thinking to control us and draw us away from a more positive reality? We have gone too long covering up these unhealthy ways of thinking. For decades, maybe centuries, the stigmas associated with mental health have been hard, if not impossible, to erase and understandably so.

Most of us have read about or have memories of relatives, friends, or ancestors who have been locked up and mistreated in mental institutions. My Uncle Lunsford was institutionalized and locked in at the Central State Hospital in Nashville. He was being treated like a wild animal. Back then (the forties and fifties and before), that is how persons with schizophrenia or other mental disorders were handled. Damaging drugs were administered just to calm patients down. No wonder fearful stigmas have developed over decades. I remember being scared to death that Uncle Lunsford would escape from the hospital, come to our house, and hurt me and my family. Unfortunately, you may have similar stories to recall about your own family history. It is my opinion that these ingrained social stigmas have thwarted the development of our society. As a result, we hesitate to seek out help and are not allowing ourselves to explore the exciting and positive possibilities that await us. There is a huge storage of wealth ahead for mental health and wholeness which we are beginning to tap into a little at a time. Let's speed up the process.

Biology – Body

Let us move on to the third important balancing triangle within the circle, Biology (The Body). I will reiterate that in order to have maximal balance, the Spirit, Mind, and Body triangles need to be operating in concert with each other. Exercise needs to be part of a balanced lifestyle along with the mental and spiritual components. Intentionally planning all of these three primary lifestyle choices is key. By balanced intentional planning, I mean not obsessing about any of these three main areas.

For example, I love to run, walk, bike, or play tennis for exercise. After exercising, I feel more alive and motivated to do the things that I want and/or need to do. My state of mind is definitely more positive and refreshed as a result. When I run, my goal is to run a 5K three times a week. A 5K is equivalent to 3.1 miles. So, 9.3 miles per week. Initially, I was impressed with half and whole marathon runners, but I know that the training involved and running the actual races do take a major toll on the body, especially the knees. Many people I know cannot run anymore due to overrunning. I want to be able to exercise for the rest of my life so that I can stay in shape and not become overweight as I age. Why are some individuals obsessed with running? Or any type of exercise for that matter? Are they running from something? These questions roll over into the psychological realm. I intentionally choose the amount of time I exercise so as not to physically exhaust myself. Some days, I go to the YMCA instead and do muscle-strengthening or go to a yoga class. My son, Andy, is a personal trainer and he has helped me with a reasonable strengthening plan. My goal is to cross-train so I will not get burned out or worn out. Again, balance is the key.

Maintaining a healthy weight is another positive by-product of exercise. I ask the question, "Why is there so much obesity?"

The answers seem fairly simple. Obsessive eating, eating unhealthy foods, not exercising, thyroid problems, and genetic disorders are some of the main culprits. On the surface, the above answers are definitely contributors; however, they can oftentimes be symptoms of deeper, conscious, or subconscious psychological reasons for obsessive eating. Our daughter, Fran, is an Integrative Nutrition Counselor and encourages us to choose or grow certain organic foods. Her website simplymindful.com contains healthy recipes and healthy lifestyle suggestions. She has a great recipe called "Cereal Bowl" which I fix just about every morning for breakfast. If you are interested, check it out.

In the last few months, I have gained between five and ten pounds which I did not want to do, so, I am headed to Weight Watchers in order to get help losing it. I need that structure because I have a hard time losing weight by myself. I find that weighing in once a week and attending the weekly Weight Watchers' meeting with others who have the same needs, contribute to my successful weight loss. I finally achieved my goal weight and plan to keep it that way. However, in the future, I will return to Weight Watchers if I need help.

8

It Begins Very Young - Children & Therapy

Between 1971 and 1984, our four children were born. Three girls and one boy. Beth in 1971, Andy and Fran in 1974, and Carolyn in 1984. It took Buddy and me ten years to recover from having a three-year-old and twins at the same time, so we waited ten years for number four. And, no, she was not a surprise for me and our children, but she was for Buddy. We wanted another baby, but Buddy was a little skeptical. He mellowed out and finally agreed with us.

Along with being determined to have a strong marriage, we were just as committed to having well-adjusted children due to the amount of mental illness in my family. Buddy and I attended a number of parent-help courses from the time our children were small through the teenage years. One class I attended was Living With Your Preschoolers, which was sponsored by The Family and Children's Service in Nashville.

Another was, Parent Effectiveness Training (P.E.T.) which Buddy and I facilitated at our church. The goal of P.E.T. is to create a democracy within the family.

Sometime during the course of Buddy's and my couple's therapy, our daughter, Fran was diagnosed with a borderline, language-based learning disability. Now it would be labeled an "alternative learning-style." She was in the sixth grade and could not keep up with her school work. As a result, Fran became extremely angry. She felt "stupid" and would verbally lash out at me when she came home from school. Again, my underlying fear of schizophrenia surfaced. I was afraid that she had it. Her struggles were also a blueprint of my own difficulty with school and feeling stupid.

Her teachers would say that Fran never caused any trouble in class and that she had many friends who loved her and helped her when she had problems with her school work. Her friends were helping her get by, and at night she was depending on Buddy and me to help her. One afternoon after school, Fran and I were on the way to her gymnastics class. She told me that she had a lot of homework to do and was afraid she would not have enough time to get it all done if she went to gymnastics.

"I. AM. NOT. GOING!" she screamed.

As I continued driving in the direction of the gym, she grabbed the steering wheel and tried to pull it down. "What are you doing?" I yelled. Fortunately, I kept the car from going off the road. I proceeded to pull over and park. We sat there quietly, and she started crying. I was thinking to myself that as soon as we got home I was going to call Dr. Spence, our pediatrician, and ask him to give me a name of a professional who could help me, Fran, and our entire family deal with her unwieldy anger.

I had called Dr. Spence a few weeks before, expressing my concerns relating to Fran's outbursts. At that time, he said that he was not too worried about it and suggested that we be patient and work it out within the family. This time was different. I knew that, as a family, we didn't have the tools required to sort it out on our own, and I knew that the only way to get through this with some degree of sanity was to seek professional help.

When I called Dr. Spence again, I told him that we nearly ran off the road as a result of Fran's outburst. This time, he took the matter more seriously and gave me the name and number of a child and family psychiatrist in the area — Dr. Ted Morton. I called Dr. Morton the next morning. His receptionist said that she would have him return my call. A few hours later, he called and said he could see us in three weeks, but if a cancellation came available, he would let me know. I did not care how long it would take. All I knew was that professional help was on the way, and that was enough.

A couple of days later, he called back and said he had a cancellation and could see me, Fran, and Buddy the next week. He explained to me that when we came, he would meet with each of us separately for a few minutes and then would get us all back together to talk.

When I hung up the phone, I let out a sigh. I was so relieved to speak to someone who knew what they were doing and had a plan as to how to get it done. The day seemed slow coming, but I did not care. I could wait.

When we met with Dr. Morton a week later, he told Buddy and me that after speaking with Fran he was impressed with her many strengths and did not feel like she needed to come back to see him unless she wanted to. My heart sank. I was shocked and happy all at the same time. But, what are we going to do about *our* problem? When he told me that Fran did not need to come back I expressed to him that I was really having a hard time with her anger and felt like, if anything, I needed to come see him. Buddy and I were meeting with a different therapist at the time. I needed to feel like I had some grasp on what was happening and I could tell Dr. Morton was the real deal. I switched therapists, and I was happy with the outcome.

Fran was halfway through the sixth grade, she was behind academically, and her self-esteem and confidence were suffering. Her teacher contacted me and recommended that she meet with Buddy and me about Fran's progress. She thought that it was best for Fran to repeat the sixth grade and preferably go to a school with smaller classrooms in order to catch up with her grade level. She said that Fran was at the top of the class socially but was at the bottom of the class academically.

I spoke to Dr. Morton about this, and he was in agreement. He told me that in an attempt to have control, many children who do not get this intervention are inclined to turn to alcohol or other drugs in high school in order to deal with their frustrations. He believed that Fran needed successes and at that moment she was experiencing a lot of failures. He said that to her, it probably feels like she is drowning and there is no help on the way, but in time she will realize the help was there right in front of her. She was extremely scared and fighting for her life. The help may not have come in the form she was expecting — moving to a new school and repeating a grade — but it was the most effective life preserver she had been thrown, and she had no other choice but to cling to it.

As expected, when Buddy and I told Fran all of this she was devastated. All hell broke loose. She yelled, "I hate everyone, Dr. Morton, Ms. Smith (her teacher), and you and Dad." No doubt, it was an unsettling time. There was a moment when Buddy wavered because it was hard for him to see her so unhappy. He was convinced she didn't need to repeat a grade just to calm things down. He could not identify with her distress. I knew deep down that repeating a grade was the right decision. Holding me back in school was the help I needed a generation before, but at the time, awareness of alternative learning styles was non-existent. I was five years old when I started the first grade and never felt like I could get ahead.

It was an uphill battle. Fran had to leave all of her friends that she loved so much, and her friends did not want her to leave. Some of them were angry with me and Buddy for taking her away from them. We understood. Adjusting to a new school and making new friends was hard. Dr. Morton had told us that children are resilient and over time, she would find her niche. He was right. We enrolled her in a non-graded Catholic school, Saint Bernard Academy, led by the Sisters of Mercy. They lived up to their name with Fran. They were merciful for her and for us. Six weeks passed by rather slowly, but Fran began to feel better. She made new friends and even became a basketball cheerleader.

Buddy began to accept the decision as he saw Fran beginning to adjust, and our peace of mind began to return. What a relief!

Many years ago I found a small piece of clay in a gift shop that read, "Children are not things to be molded, but are people to be unfolded." No name was under the quote, but it summarizes my basic philosophy about children. Children are free spirits, and they need guidance and love. In the many parenting classes I've taught and attended, I've learned that as parents, we often want to control and mold our children because we, ourselves, were controlled and molded. This needs to change. The cycle needs to be broken. One of my main objectives in this book is to explain — from my seventy-seven years of experience in this world as a daughter, a sister, a mother, a wife, and a grandmother — how I believe this can be done. I believe that there is a huge difference between healthy guidance and direction and unhealthy control and manipulation. I want to share these experiences where I have tried to resist the mold, resist any kind of manipulation to get my children into that mold, and to help them pave their own path.

Artist Unknown

Buddy and I know the value, both for ourselves and for our children, of playing and participating with them and their friends at an early age and as they grow up. In other words, having FUN together. Quality relationships, both within and outside the family were a priority. I believe our children developed a love for people by asking friends to come home with them after school, by participating in extracurricular activities such as sports and inviting a friend to go with them to the beach for spring break, etc.

I want to elaborate on beach trips. Each friend's parents would give us spending money for their child. Thanks to our generous beach-condo-owning friends and family members, we just had to pay the week's cleaning fee, which definitely helped to make it all possible. The endeavor with extra children was definitely extra effort and responsibility for Buddy and me, but we found that allowing our children to bring a friend along enabled us to know their friends better and for them to know us. Actually having a "buddy" made the trip more fun and easier for all of us. By so doing, we were trying to send the message to our children that we like and care about their friends. Hopefully, they felt respected and trusted. That was our main goal in addition to having a blast and getting a tan. So, enjoy your children as much as you can and make plans with the people you value, including yourself.

I found value in reading Susan Ariel Rainbow Kennedy's (SARK's) poem, "How to Really Love a Child." I think it beautifully expands on the clay mold I found years ago. It is an instruction manual for that notion and helps jog our memory about how un-boxlike a child's mind is. Sark so eloquently expresses the value of small things in life that cannot be purchased. Simple pleasures. Intangible becomes tangible.

It's easy to think there isn't enough time to let things unfold. Molding can seem easier and be less time-consuming. But I encourage us to slow down and ask ourselves, am I in charge of my schedule, or is my schedule in charge of me? Give yourself time to think and plan what you value. Centering one's priorities around interpersonal relationships takes time and intentional planning and cannot be a rush job. Don't be thrown around by your schedule. Consciously make it yourself, and make room for a social life for you and for your children, even if it takes more work. The benefits are invaluable for everyone.

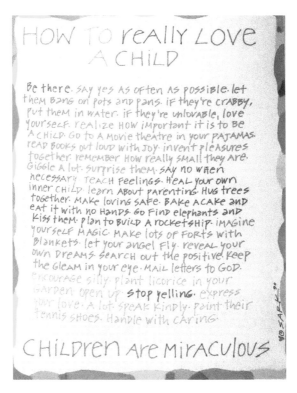

©SARK, reprinted with permission
1990

I also questioned the molding that took place at church. Our children's spiritual development was very important to Buddy and me, so having a healthy and positive church/faith experience was a priority. Beth, Fran, Andy, and Carolyn started in the church nursery as soon as our pediatrician gave us the green light. They received much love and a sense of well-being there. During the worship service, the nursery and preschoolers stayed in childcare while their parents attended the service. When children became first graders, the church staff suggested decided that it was time for them to attend the worship service with their parents. This was where Buddy and I and the church differed in our thinking. Our children did not like sitting still that long and we did not want to force them to do so. I started thinking about ways in which we could re-shape this experience. Surely we weren't the only family with antsy six-year-olds. And again, we wanted them to have good feelings about the church, so I came up with an idea. With the permission of the church staff, I started what was called an "extended session," where children, with their parent's permission, attended the first part of the worship service with their families and then left to play and skate with their peers in the gymnasium during the remainder of the service. The parents of those children who participated would rotate supervising them. As our children got older, they could choose to stay in the worship service with me and Buddy, choose to help in the extended session or help in the nursery.

I believe our children developed a more positive view of church, a love and respect for little ones, a stronger relationship with their peers, and an appreciation for their friends' parents. It took more time and energy to develop a new routine, but everyone won. This was my interpretation and my effort toward "unfolding" — listening to my children's wishes and taking them seriously. Not getting stubborn or increasingly angry at our children's resistance, but remaining open to what they were trying to say. I found this very important and especially so in the early years when our children were at such impressionable ages. I believe Buddy and I were trusting their intelligence, and they sensed this trust. Experiencing trustworthiness is so important for all of us.

Physical fitness and health are other primary values for our family. Buddy and I would put the kids — even as infants — in a red wagon and participate in local "fun runs" and 5-K's. We had a blast! I am proud to say that we are still participating in some of these events during Thanksgiving and Christmas. We round up friends in our neighborhood to go with us. Playing outside was what we did even in the rain and the snow. Tree-climbing, swing sets, balls, balloons, dome climber, sandbox, seesaws, badminton, ping pong, bubbles, sports, slip and slide, tennis, water-play, sprinklers, baby pool, parachutes, umbrellas, sleds, treehouse, hose swing, zipline, hammock, having fun... The list of outdoor fun is endless. These activities aren't new to adults, but they are to children. Oh, to see and feel with the senses of a child!

While questioning the mold and listening to our children's needs, Buddy and I found that it was important to be in tune with them and ourselves mentally, physically, and spiritually. So, in a nutshell, we did, and are still doing, our best to nourish ourselves, our children, and grandchildren in those ways. We are happy to see them doing the same.

The Rudolph Red Nose Run, 1988
Left to right: Fran, Andy, Me, Carolyn, Buddy, and Elysabeth

9

The Importance of Taking Action

I am too aware of the suicides — of all ages — that have occurred and continue to occur. I recently read that middle school-aged suicides are at an all-time high. I understand that in most cases the underlying issue is clinical depression. This is an intergenerational and international crisis that must be tackled and prevented. Since these tortuous states of mind can be alleviated and transformed, how can we break this negative cycle of mental dis-ease and useless deaths?

Tackling such a feat feels analogous to the process of unknotting a knotted chain. This is a task I believe we can all identify with. Let's say you want to wear this nice chain, but it is full of knots, a cluttered mess. Loosening and untying the knots is a real pain and doing so, takes a considerable amount of time. Who really wants or has the time to do it? But, you know if you do not take that time, the necklace stays knotted up and virtually useless. If you *do* take the time, the necklace becomes useful and pleasing to wear. The final product is so rewarding — a sense of success, freedom, and relief ensues.

Emotionally speaking, which should we choose to do? Stay knotted up and cluttered in our emotions and thoughts or become freer, looser, and untangled? Whether we know it or not, we do have that choice when it comes to our states of mind. However, we may feel so knotted and tangled up that we do not even know we have a choice. I believe that such strong and uncontrollable feelings of desperation and dead ended-ness can lead to extreme depression and/or suicide if not recognized by oneself, a friend, a therapist, a parent, and/or a loved one. As I've stated before, I believe a Higher Power gave humankind the ability to study religion and to study the mind and each of these entities can serve as a complement to the other and not as a threat.

When things reach a point of emotional desperation, I believe that rapid psychological intervention is necessary. Many persons of faith think the answer is "to pray." Yes, we can pray. My belief system informs me that immediate psychological resources are a part of answered prayer. I believe that our Higher Power has provided us access to these resources through therapy. God has given us the ability to learn and understand. God has given us other people, who have spent their lives learning and understanding things we might never know about. Prayer is definitely important and is one of the many ways God is helping us. In that regard, I believe in seeking out persons who have spent their lives studying human behavior and the mind. Individuals who are trained to heal by incorporating science and compassion. Ministers, priests, rabbis, friends, etc. can be supportive and well-intended, but if they are not also well-trained psychologically to deal with the depth of therapy necessary, then positive outcomes can quickly fall through the cracks and circumstances can go south very rapidly.

Dynamic clinical psychotherapy enables an individual to go back into their past and understand why distortions have developed. When one goes back into their past to understand the depth of their sadness and the reason distortions in thinking happen, it is not until then that permanent change in one's state of mind and quality of life begins to occur. By putting a name on the problem, one's self-esteem is enhanced. The emotional spiral starts going up instead of down. If we fall short and miss such an opportunity to use these extravagant gifts our Creator has given us, it is incredibly unfortunate. These gifts are the answers to our prayers.

My husband, Buddy, is an ordained United Methodist minister. He graduated from Vanderbilt Divinity School. Part of his divinity degree included some psychological therapy and pastoral counseling courses. He was not trained to the extent that he could practice in-depth therapy or even come close to doing so. Most spiritual counselors are dedicated, passionate, and caring, and their intentions and motivations are good and very appreciated. However, more in-depth psychological training is absolutely necessary. Some clients and/or pastoral counselors do not want to recognize this factor for one reason or another. The client continues spiritual or pastoral therapy, and many times the pastoral counselor does not refer the vulnerable client to a more qualified psychotherapist. Unfortunately, too little progress is made over too long a period of time, and issues such as depression, divorce, suicide, etc. do occur.

One certainly does not have to get to such a dire position as the examples mentioned above. Prevention, if not elimination, of extreme discomfort, is my goal. As I mentioned earlier, when I first met with my therapist, Dr. Morton, I thought I was in pretty good shape. I realize now that I was pretty clueless and needed to work on my own self-worth. I can now reflect on the profound and healthy changes that I am thankfully experiencing due to choosing a clinical therapist and sticking with it. I can more successfully live and enjoy my life in the present and not live so much in the past and future. The grass is greener, the sky is bluer, stars are brighter, grandchildren are even "funner," my relationships are more positive and healthier. As a result of all the hard work that I and my therapist have done over the years, life gets better and better. My struggles have not totally gone away, and I know they never will, but I am in a better state of mind to cope with them whatever they are and however they present themselves.

I only wish that I had begun therapy earlier in my life when I was in my teens, twenties, or thirties instead of my forties. Hopefully, those who read my book will consider doing so — the earlier, the better. The main reason for psychotherapy is to improve self-esteem. No one needs to be afraid due to the stigmas associated with mental illness. During one of our sessions, Dr. Morton said, "The individuals who will benefit most from your therapy are your grandchildren." Wow, what an investment. I thought he was going to say that my own children and I would receive the most benefit.

Because of all of the time I put into understanding the complexity of my mental state, I feel weightless. The famous song, "I Believe I Can Fly" by R. Kelly, best describes the freedom I experience when I am untethered from fear and self-doubt.

"I believe I can fly. I believe I can touch the sky!"

10

My Therapy Begins

Dr. Ted Morton's approach to psychotherapy is referred to as dynamic psychotherapy — dynamic, meaning "ongoing" — and I would see him on a regular basis for an indefinite amount of visits. At his suggestion, I scheduled an hourly appointment once a week. Each visit was one hundred dollars, and our insurance covered half of it. That amount was not affordable for us, but the way I looked at it, we could not afford *not* to afford it.

After a few weekly therapy sessions, Dr. Morton explained that I needed to work on my self-esteem. I did not think anything was wrong with my self-esteem, but I figured that he was the professional and knew what he was talking about.

As I progressed, my appointments were every other week and eventually became once a month. I found that this style of therapy really worked well for me. Dr. Morton told me that he takes a proactive approach as opposed to a passive one. Instead of telling me what to do, he would give me suggestions alongside my ideas, which would allow me room to make my own decisions. I did not have to work so hard to figure everything out for myself. What a relief! This does not mean by any stretch of the imagination that I did not struggle. I struggled a lot. But it was productive. It felt like a fall with a parachute instead of an uncontrollable drop. For the first time, I felt what a strong third-party support felt like. I never knew such a thing existed. Ted and I made a good team.

Dr. Morton's first name, "Ted," became a household name around our house. I told everyone in our family that we all had a standing appointment once a month with a family psychiatrist, and if anyone wanted to talk with him regarding an issue they had, he would make himself available. I knew that normalizing therapy and counseling was vital. I wanted our family to consider it as a preventative routine, just like going to the dentist to get your teeth cleaned or getting a physical from your doctor. Deep down, I knew that I would be the primary appointment attendee, and that was fine with me. At least all family members had a heads up and knew that support was there. The negative stigmas associated with mental illness must change for our overall well-being, and I have been dedicated to imparting that to my kids and grandkids. In order for the next generation to get the emotional help they need, we must do all we can to weave it into the fabric of our lives.

After a few appointments, Dr. Morton recommended that I consider taking the antidepressant, Prozac. He diagnosed me as having biological depression. He explained that Prozac was not addictive — I could stop taking it whenever I wanted to — and that it would take a couple of weeks for me to start feeling the effects. At first, I was reluctant to take that type of drug but I trusted Dr. Morton's evaluation. He added that my mood swings would improve so, I decided to go for it.

As the two-week mark approached, I started feeling calmer and more confident. I noticed that I became kinder to myself, my family, and my friends. Today, I still take a generic form of Prozac and have never regretted that decision. When I first met with Dr. Morton, it was an adventure into the unknown. I was forty and pregnant with our fourth child, Carolyn. Today, I am seventy-seven years old. We met consistently once a month for twenty-five years. He retired ten years ago. The most important benefit of my therapy with Dr. Morton was that he enabled me, through his psychological expertise, to develop independence and confidence. At the beginning of our work together he said that I needed to work on my self-worth, and he was right. For a long time, I was dependent upon him and others to unravel my past but, over time, he enabled me to think for myself, to think more positively of myself, and to love myself and others with confidence. As a result, my unhealthy dependence upon him, and others began to wane. By the time he retired, our work together allowed me to feel as if my tangled chain had been untangled. I do miss him but in a healthy, positive, constructive way.

In hindsight, it took running off the side of the road to get on the right track. I thought it was going to be my daughter that needed the most help but in the end, it was an opportunity to help her, to help myself, and to help our family. It was the beginning of a significant period of growth for all of us.

It's the best money I have ever spent. I will continue to spend it with my new therapist, once or twice a month, depending on my emotional needs. Because I cannot be objective when it comes to myself, I believe in the importance of a trained therapist who can help me be objective. Friends can help do this to some degree but, I don't want to wear them out. Sometimes it feels like I'm spinning my wheels trying to get advice from friends.

This incredible transformational therapy has been invaluable to me, my marriage, my relationships with my children, grandchildren, and many others. Mission accomplished, Ted! We worked hard and it paid off many times over. I love you and I thank you!

11

Finding a Therapist

If you've never seen a therapist before, it is hard to know where to begin. It has taken me many years to slowly unravel what I have liked and not liked about certain therapists' approaches and hone in on what has been effective for me. As I said, Buddy and I saw a psychologist prior to our therapy sessions with Dr. Morton. We needed help due to our difficulties with our daughter and within our own relationship. The previous therapist's approach was more passive, meaning he would do a lot of listening, and we would do most of the talking. There was very little input on his part.

Dr. Morton was a proactive therapist. There was more dialogue between us and he offered suggestions for us to think about. Buddy and I were to consider his input and make our own decisions. We were not stewing in our own minds as to what decisions we needed to make. His suggestions were invaluable. We were so relieved to have his professional and proactive support.

One thing I had to learn was that if your therapist doesn't seem to be a good fit, you must not be shy or hesitant to move on to someone else. I told Dr. Morton that I was embarrassed to tell our previous psychologist that I would be going to another therapist. He helped me feel less guilty about it and emphasized that choosing a therapist is about what is right for you, not them. Even though one develops a personal relationship with a therapist, it is important to remember that if it's not working, there is no need to pay them more money just to be polite. He suggested I nicely call it quits, and that is what I did.

Not long ago, a friend from San Diego called and expressed her need for finding a therapist. Fortunately, she had insurance because good therapy can be expensive without it. I have discovered that some highly recommended therapists do not take insurance and make therapy financially prohibitive for many. However, some of those therapists will take out-of-network clients, and the client's insurance company will reimburse a significant amount of the fee. There are therapists though, who take full insurance and will be listed under an insurance plan. My therapist, Dr. Morton was that type of therapist, thank God.

Now, the big question is which therapist would be a good fit? Before researching those therapists online, I suggested that she call her primary care physician, and ask for recommendations. Next, I suggested that she check out the names of providers which are listed in her insurance booklet and research their credentials. Also, I told her that the *Psychology Today* website is an excellent resource. Most of the therapists will have their own web page where they give a description of the type of therapy they specialize in. I also recommended that my friend center in on the clinical psychologists or licensed clinical social workers (LCSW) who practiced dynamic psychotherapy. The clinical title is critical due to the more extensive training they receive. In addition, sometimes the psychologists are rated by their clients on the website. This can also be helpful in making a decision.

When you think you are as satisfied as much as you can be with your choice, make an appointment. Note that some insurance companies require a referral from a primary care physician in order to make an appointment, but many don't have that stipulation. Go to a few sessions to get a sense of the dynamic between the two of you. Never, and I do mean never, remain with a therapist if you do not feel he or she is a good match. You will be wasting your time, money, energy, and your life. Do not feel embarrassed to change if the chemistry is not working. In time, you will find the right therapist, and you will know it. What all this comes down to is that the client feels good about the relationship they have with the therapist and that significant progress is being made.

If an individual does not have insurance, then I suggest finding a therapy center like The Family and Children's Service in Nashville. A non-profit organization like this can provide therapy using a sliding scale based on your income.

Also, a highly recommended pastoral counseling center would be another option. The reason I shy away from church counseling centers is that some of them push religion too much. But, if you have a good friend who is level-headed and she/he highly recommends a particular therapist at a mainstream church counseling center, that is great. Again, if you do not notice significant progress, move on to someone else.

For updated 2019-2020 professional clarity, it is my understanding that a psychiatrist's role, who is a medical doctor, primarily diagnoses and prescribes medications. A clinical psychologist does "talk therapy." This is all new for me because my therapist, Dr. Morton, a psychiatrist, diagnosed medications for me *and* we did "talk therapy." For the most part, the way it works now is that the clinical psychologist and the psychiatrist confer with each other in order to determine the correct medication for their client if that is needed.

For a short period of time, I was working with a clinical psychologist who was recommended to me by a friend. After approximately eight excellent sessions, I decided that I needed concentrated help with aging issues. My therapist was in his forties and admitted that aging was not his specialty. My husband is aging faster than I, and this is very hard for me. As a result, I am experiencing feelings of depression and know that I am in need of a better understanding of the aging process. Also, I am afraid to die and don't want to die. The therapist I was seeing recommended someone else, and I am productively working on my aging issues with her.

12

Where We Go From Here

The TENNESSEAN
January 7, 2021

Associated Press
"Protestors supporting President Donald Trump stormed the U.S. Capital on Wednesday, clashing with police and forcing a delay in the constitutional process to affirm President-elect Joe Biden's win."

USA Today Network – Tennessee
"Most of Tennessee's Republican delegation began the day vowing to support President Donald Trump's futile efforts to overturn the results of the 2020 presidential election, saying they would not certify several states' Electoral College votes."

As terrible as this insurrection was, the onslaught illuminated to the world the varying degrees of imbalance in the United States. This unrest has been growing for generations and in my opinion, the vastness of that unrest directly corresponds to the magnitude of disregard towards the culprit – mental illness. These events are a part of the silent mental illness pandemic, which is beginning to not be so silent. We've been in denial of the mental illness issues in this country, and due to the stigmas surrounding them, we have allowed these issues to perpetuate over time. Our denial must end and the stigmas must be disarmed if we are to save our democracy.

This is very serious business. We are in grave territory. You and I must take responsibility for what is going on and do something about it. I do not want to alarm anyone, but I will. The silent pandemic has created a state of emergency — a crisis — and it's time to be alarmed. This book is an effort to call that pandemic by name, and in naming it, we are acknowledging the deep-seated issues of mental illness in all of its complicated forms. Doing so clears the pathway for us to start dealing with it in rational and informed ways.

In the *Tree of Life: Multiple Global Pandemics* shown on the next page, I have drawn a tree to represent the effects of untreated mental illness. The trunk of the tree represents the long-standing and deep-rooted nature of this silent pandemic. I believe that mental illness is the source from which these destructive worldly circumstances come. The branches and vines depict the negative and deadly issues that we are currently dealing with. These avoidable appendages are threatening the health of our world.

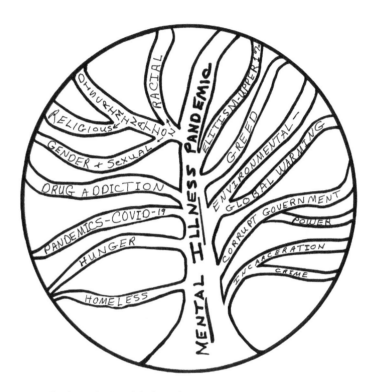

Tree of Life: Multiple Global Pandemics

Monumental changes must occur if we are to reverse this invasive growth. Educators and government officials need to be trained in how to deal with mental health issues and be willing to turn to medical professionals for guidance moving forward. Not only do we need this commitment from our educators and leaders, but we must also take a personal oath to invest in our own mental well-being and become leaders of change.

It is my opinion that the mental illness pandemic supersedes COVID-19 and that the complications arising from this widespread virus, are a result of on-going psychological neglect. Due to our country being unprepared for the arrival of COVID-19, hundreds of thousands of people have died and continue to die. If the Pandemic Task Force had been able to continue doing its job, many, if not most of these deaths, could have been prevented. It is no surprise that we are anxious, distressed, and depressed. Both pandemics are, directly and indirectly, stemming from the decades or even centuries-old lack of attention to the visible and invisible mental illness issues we are experiencing today and have been, across our globe, for so, so long.

On February 23, 2020, a twenty-six-year-old black man, Ahmaud Arbery, was innocently jogging in his Georgia neighborhood. According to the news, a white father and his son were stalking him in their truck and killed him with a shotgun. This event was not publicly announced until three months later when a video was disclosed. It is now labeled as a racial hate crime. To follow-through with such a horrendous act suggests to me that the perpetrators' minds are distorted and full of hate. People all over the world, due to the color of their skin, religious beliefs, nationality, sexual orientation, and many other reasons, are being targeted. When are we, as a world, going to understand why mental illness is so abundant? It is incredibly tragic and sad and we must understand the source of these issues.

Not long after Ahmaud's video was made public, a policeman pressed his knee into George Floyd's neck while Floyd was screaming, "I cannot breathe." Another officer was holding his legs down. Two other policemen were watching all of this while George Floyd was strangled to death. This is analogous to the brutal "lynchings" that occurred in the thirties, forties, and fifties. Absolutely horrific. After these tragic deaths, many more have occurred. Racism is yet another result of worldwide mental distortion.

Some people might ask, "Why is our Higher Power allowing all of these disastrous events to happen?" Well, we need not look further than ourselves. Our Higher Power is sadder than we are about these situations. Seeing all of these horrendous events, that some in our society have caused and/ or chosen to participate in, are hard to bear. Many have chosen to "See No Evil, Hear No Evil, and Speak No Evil," and take no action. Inaction and denial are choices. Martin Luther King said, "To ignore evil is to become an accomplice to it" — I agree.

We might think we are victims of these unfathomable circumstances, but we aren't. We must evaluate our priorities, come to terms with our values, and take action accordingly. We cannot rely on others to assume this responsibility for us. Each person needs to decide for themselves where they go from here.

I just returned from a power walk in my neighborhood. A major thought surfaced — a serendipity. Twenty years or so ago in a therapy session I told my psychiatrist that three things were really working well for me. First was my regular sessions with him. The second was exercise. And third, was my daily devotions and spiritual growth. His response was, "Keep doing what you are doing." Well, I have followed his advice even though I've felt overwhelmed, depressed, and unmotivated at times. I've chosen to take action and hold myself accountable to my values.

From working with my psychiatrist, I've also learned that it is imperative to replace negative and untrue thoughts about myself with positive ones. Negative thoughts like *I'm being selfish* or *I'm being self-centered* can be exchanged with, *I trust, and believe in myself.* I have found that it is crucial and necessary to center on myself for periods of time and not consider it selfish. By directing my focus inward, I am more capable and freer to live and think more positively. I become oriented to my needs, and as a result, I am in a better position to be of help and support to my family, friends, and neighbors. Our bodies are holy temples and we are created to take care of them. When we take time for ourselves, everyone benefits.

I hope and pray that you and I and the whole world will see positive and healthy changes begin to happen. In the meantime, beyond a shadow of a doubt, I know that an ever-present Higher Power is within all human beings and is surrounding us with comfort, guidance, strength, power, and balance. We are meant to be in partnership with our Higher Power. Many have chosen not to tap into these gifts for one reason or another. Eventually, goodness will prevail. Our higher power is in charge. Let us be confident and appreciate these invaluable and unconditional gifts from God. May we never forget them, may we always remember.

~

"Dismiss all anxiety from your minds; instead, present your needs to God through prayer and petition, giving thanks for all circumstances. Then God's own peace, which is beyond all understanding, will stand guard over your hearts and minds."

Philippians 4: 6-7, in a letter written by the apostle Paul to the Christian church in Phillipi

The Inclusive Bible: The First Egalitarian Translation

9 780578 796383